SEW!

A complete guide for sewing today

MYRA COLES

Heinemann Professional Publishing

◆ SEW! ◆

My thread I have, my pattern too,
And fabric by the yard,
Lining, zip and shoulder pads,
Six buttons on a card.
My shears are sharp, the iron's hot,
The pressing cloth to hand –
My machine is threaded, set to go,
The sewing sequence planned.

If you can't sew – you'll never know
The joys I've pictured here:
Of craft and creation, of complete dedication,
And sew on ... year after year!

MYRA COLES

Heinemann Professional Publishing Ltd
Halley Court, Jordan Hill, Oxford OX2 8EJ

OXFORD   LONDON   MELBOURNE   AUCKLAND   SINGAPORE
IBADAN   NAIROBI   GABORONE   KINGSTON

First published 1989

British Library Cataloguing in Publication Data
Coles, Myra
Sew!: a complete guide for sewing today.
1. Sewing – Amateurs' manuals
I. Title
646.2

ISBN 0 434 90257 8

Cover photographs by McCabe

Printed in Singapore by
Imago Publishing Ltd

CONTENTS

FOREWORD

Over the years, Myra has made many valuable contributions to home sewing. Her vast technical knowledge of both sewing and the sewing machine has enabled her to tailor the contents of this, her third book, to the special needs of all home sewers.

She has imparted all her home sewing knowledge, aiming to enlighten, stimulate and communicate the expertise necessary to give a professional finish on garments or craft items.

This book will guide both beginners and expert home sewers through a comprehensive understanding and appreciation of sewing. It informs the reader about products available to achieve a perfect finish; it explains about fabrics and patterns; it describes techniques applicable to every sewing situation and ends with a section aptly named 'Finishing Touches' for those interested in crafts of various kinds.

Myra's first two successful publications have become working manuals for all sewing machine owners and this book should become the definitive text for all home sewers.

David Knowles
Managing Director, Tootal Craft

PREFACE

This book is for sewers from beginners to City and Guilds standard – and the experienced sewer will also find much useful advice on modern machines and techniques.

The aim has been to provide a positive guide. The text takes the sewer step by step through equipment needs, how to interpret pattern instructions, choosing and understanding fabrics, and using haberdashery. There is a full guide to stitches and techniques on the sewing machine, and ideas and instructions for assembling garments.

The language is down-to-earth and non-technical, and the book explodes the myth that only involved and time-consuming methods will give good results.

ACKNOWLEDGEMENTS

My sincere thanks to the following, who supplied help, encouragement, information and photographs:

International Institute for Cotton
21 Cavendish Place, London W1M 9DL

International Linen
31 Great Queen Street, London WC2B 5AA

International Mohair Association
28 Albermarle Street, London W1X 3FA

Home Laundering Consultative Council
7 Swalled Place, London W1R 7AA

European Commission for the Promotion of Silk
50 Upper Brook Street, London W1Y 1PG

International Wool Secretariat
Wool House, Carlton Gardens, London SW1Y 5AE

British Wool Marketing Board
Oak Mills, Station Road, Clayton, Bradford BD14 6JD

Tootal Craft
56 Oxford Street, Manchester

Swish Products Ltd
Tamworth, Staffordshire

ICI Fibres
Publications Unit, Harrogate, Yorkshire

Vilene Organisation
PO Box 3, Greetland, Halifax HX4 8NJ

Liberty of London
Regent's Street, London W1R 6AH

Alexander Fabrics
32 Wentworth Street, London E1

Samuel Tweed
Whitley Willows Mill, Lepton, Huddersfield, West Yorkshire

Rufflet
Sharston Road, Wythenshaw, Manchester M22 4TH

McCabe Photography
Crown Street Studio, Hebden Bridge, West Yorkshire

Newey Goodman Ltd
Sedgeley Road West, Tipton, West Midlands DY4 8AH

Sewing Machine Trader Association
24 Fairlawn Grove, Chiswick, London W4 5EH

Bernina Sewing Machines
50/2 Great Sutton Street, London EC1V 0DJ

Elna Sewing Machines (GB) Ltd
180/2 Tottenham Court Road, London W1P 9LE

Frister Rossmann Sewing Machines Ltd
Old Mill Road, Portishead, Bristol BS20 9BX

Jones & Brother Sewing Machine Company
Guide Bridge, Audenshaw, Manchester M34 5JD

New Home Sewing Machine Company
Cromwell Road, Bredbury, Stockport, Cheshire

Pfaff Britain Ltd
Pfaff House, East Street, Leeds LS9 8EH

Singer Sewing Machine Company
Unit H, Graton Way, West Ham Industrial Estate, Basingstoke, Hampshire

Riccar Sewing Machine Company
Nuffield Way, Abingdon, Oxfordshire

Viking Husqvarna Sewing Machine Company
Oakly Road, Luton, Bedfordshire

Viscount Sewing Machines
Unit 6, City Industrial Park, West Quay Road, Southampton

IKEA of Warrington

I offer particular thanks to my good friends and colleagues in the sewing machine companies: your continued help, support and enthusiasm for my projects is very much appreciated.

Especial thanks also to the following:

David Knowles and Tootal Craft, who freely supplied copious amounts of thread and haberdashery for samples.

Liberty of London, who generously supplied fabrics.

Maggie Swain, for making up various beautiful samples for this book and for her unfailing support and enthusiasm.

Gerald and Sue Harris, for welcoming us into their home, where we took many of the beautiful photographs, and for their continued encouragement with all my projects.

Stan McCabe, whose expert photography has enhanced the pages of this book and whose patience and enthusiasm was always appreciated.

Bryan, who spent untold hours assisting me with the research and index for *Sew!* and for proof checking with me at various stages. His patience and zeal have been invaluable both to me and to this book.

TOOLS AND WORKSPACE

Good equipment is essential for the modern workroom. Some items are general sewing requisites; some are needed to alter patterns and plot and plan our craft designs accurately and geometrically. Some are available from good haberdashery departments and specialist shops, and others from stationers or art shops. You may not need every single item listed – but I suggest a number of good alternatives.

◆ SCISSORS

◇ *Shears* for cutting out.
◇ *All-purpose* for cutting paper, patterns and so on.
◇ *Dressmaking* for general fabric and thread cutting.
◇ *Embroidery* for fine work, appliqué, cut work and so on.
◇ *Snips* for thread trimming.

Always keep your scissors in good condition: *never* use your fabric scissors to cut paper or anything other than fabric or threads. Investing in really good scissors pays dividends, and you will get many years of use from them.

◆ PINS

◇ *Glass-headed* pins are excellent for dressmaking, housecraft and general craft work. Their large heads make them so easy to pull from the pinpad – yet they are fine enough for most fabrics.
◇ *Wedding-dress and lace* pins are for exceptionally fine use.
◇ *Ballpoint* pins are ideal for knitted and jersey fabrics.

I recommend a large pincushion. A wrist pincushion for use during trying on is a most useful addition – and so is a magnet in case of upsets!

◆ MEASURING

◇ *Tape measure* Choose a good fibreglass tape measure. Because measuring must be exact and accurate, this should be replaced at least every two years.
◇ *Yardstick or metrestick* This is useful for measuring fabric, checking hems and so on, and is required for drafting and pattern alteration.
◇ *Perspex ruler, set square and curved ruler* These are required for drafting and pattern alteration.

◆ MARKING

◇ *Tailor's chalk* In a variety of different colours.
◇ *Chalk pencils* In a variety of colours.
◇ *Tracing wheel and carbon paper* To transfer markings from a master design.
◇ *Embroidery pen/pencil* A selection is available, with various means of removing the marks on completion. For marking designs and also for construction points.
◇ *Felt-tip pens and various pencils* These have 1001 uses: choose a colourful range.

1.1 Equipment (McCabe)

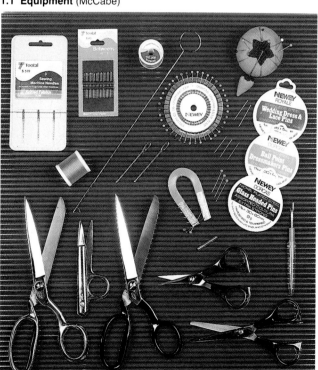

1.2 Measuring and marking (McCabe)

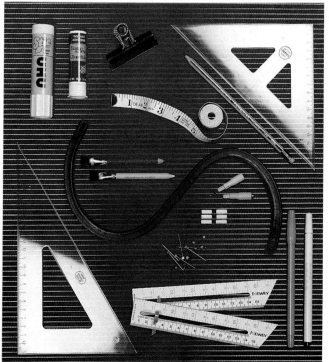

◆ PAPER

A selection of squared paper, graph paper and pattern tissue is required for planning, plotting graphs and designing, and for pattern amendments and alterations.

◆ ADHESIVES

Fabric glue, glue sticks, aerosols and so on are required for craft and appliqué work. A good choice is available in stores and specialist shops.

◆ CUTTING-OUT BOARD

This is a large work surface to lay over a table, on the carpet or even over a bed. It is graded into squares, and shows bias lines, straight of grain lines and various curves.

◆ WORKING CONDITIONS

You can only work well and comfortably if everything is to hand. If you are lucky enough to have a sewing room, plan it as well as you would a fitted kitchen. If your work area is a dining-room or kitchen, the equipment can still be arranged around you in logical positions whilst you are working.

The actual sewing position is important. A firm table or cabinet is an absolute necessity for your sewing machine, and it should be at a sensible height. Never balance the machine on the edge of a coffee table. Your chair is most important too. It should be complementary to the height of the table – the machine must not be under your chin – and the foot pedal must be at a comfortable reach. The average height of 750 mm for a sewing table is definitely too high for smaller people; if necessary, buy a solid table for your machine and cut the legs to the right length!

Good lighting is most important – especially if you have to sew at night or if your room is naturally dark. Invest in spotlights to illuminate your work area.

◆ IRONING

The ironing board is also very important. An ideal model will adjust to *any* height – but the board should be adjustable to a variety of heights at least.

A surprising amount of work can be done on the ironing board. It is the perfect work surface for very many jobs, often being more suitable than a slippery table. The padded surface is so useful for assembling your garments because you can pin into the padding to hold fabrics exactly where you want them. Details such as tucks and pleats are so much easier done in this way, and of course they can be pressed immediately *before* moving the fabric.

The type of iron – steam or dry – is a personal choice: there are excellent examples of both on the market. If possible have both types – but ensure that you have a good point or 'toe' to the iron for getting into tricky little places. A pressing cloth, to use wet or dry, is essential. Again various types can be purchased, but a large piece of butter muslin is ideal.

A sleeve board is useful to press small areas – sleeves, of course, children's clothes and various craft items.

An ironing press will give extremely professional results on many pressing jobs, and it is a good additional piece of equipment in dressmaking and craft work.

Everything you stitch needs to be pressed: do not stint on this essential piece of equipment.

THE SEWING MACHINE

The machine is probably the most expensive piece of sewing equipment that you will ever purchase. Take time and care to investigate the various machines on the market. Have them demonstrated and try them out for yourself in the store or specialist shop. Always buy the very best that you can afford. As with other major items, the standard will improve with the price – and so will the quality of your stitching.

Sewing machines fall into various categories, no matter who the manufacturer is or where they are made. To cope with modern fabrics, to get quick results and to simplify your stitching it is ideal to have a free-arm machine with a variety of stitches for utility work (putting garments and other items together) which should include some stretch and overcasting stitches. The top-quality machines will automatically include some fancy or embroidery stitches. Do not be put off by the inclusion of these, because they do not make the machine more difficult or complicated to use – and, when you become fully conversant with your machine, these stitches will often prove useful. The professional finish of the stitching on these machines, even on the basic stitches or patterns, will normally be excellent.

◆ MACHINE TYPES

There are two basic types of machine:

◇ *Flat-bed machines* will do limited sewing and are normally at the lower end of the price range. They are the traditional type to fit into a sewing cabinet (although manufacturers have now designed some cabinets for free-arm machines). Flat-bed machines are often (but not exclusively) heavy, and for some specialist tasks this can be advantageous.

◇ *Free-arm machines* are often also called sleeve-arm machines. Most sewers favour this type of machine for dressmaking, children's wear and craft work because the slim arm under the needle makes sewing collars, cuffs, trousers, armholes, sleeves and curved seams very much easier. The sewing area can be made larger either by adjusting the built-in movable base plate or by attaching a separate extension plate. Both designs are simple to use.

◆ **PRINCIPLES OF OPERATION**

The machines can then be categorized according to the principles of operation, as follows.

Basic machine

Usually this is a flat-bed model. It will only do very limited work, namely the straight stitch and sometimes a zigzag stitch (Figure 1.3).

Semi-automatic

This machine offers a few more stitches by the movement of various levers or dials on the face of the machine. Additional stitches can include stretch stitch, blind hem and sometimes limited decorative stitches. Sometimes too, it can include a semi-automatic four-stage buttonhole.

These machines will normally have the stitch pattern cams built into the mechanism; each stitch will have its own cam. Some models have the cams supplied in a separate box, and the user inserts the correct cam according to the stitch required.

Fully automatic

These machines always have the pattern cams built in, and the user/operator merely selects the required stitch with the pattern selector (Figure 1.4). A medium-priced machine will usually include a selection of utility stitches, decorative

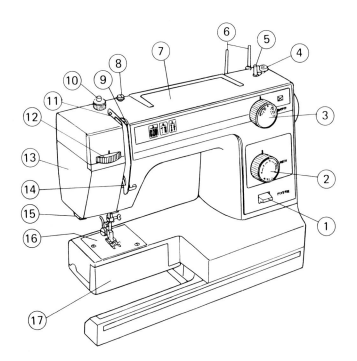

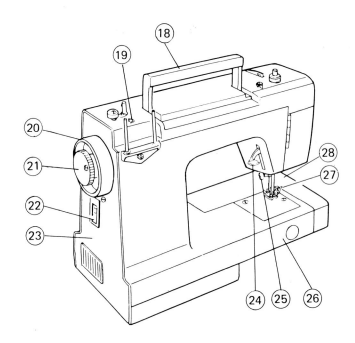

1	Reverse stitch lever	11	Thread guide	21	Stop motion knob
2	Stitch length dial	12	Thread tension dial	22	Machine socket
3	Pattern selector dial	13	Face plate	23	Belt cover
4	Bobbin winder stopper	14	Check spring holder	24	Presser foot lifter
5	Bobbin winder spindle	15	Thread cutter	25	Needle clamp screw
6	Spool pins	16	Needle plate	26	Free arm
7	Top cover	17	Hook cover	27	Presser foot
8	Bobbin winder thread guide	18	Carrying handle	28	Extension table (Accessory storage box)
9	Thread take-up lever	19	Thread guide		
10	Pressure regulator	20	Balance wheel		

1.3 Example of a basic free-arm machine

stitches, automatic buttonhole and so on. As the price rises so does the number of stitches and techniques and the quality of the stitch.

To produce stretch stitches, the feed dog moves the fabric backwards and forwards as the needle darts from side to side, thus putting a reverse stitch into the seam or embroidery. Embroidery stitches that include this reverse stitching are ideal for use on all types of stretch fabrics.

Other features to look for within this range of machines are variable needle positions; an extra wide needle swing; a full rotary hook; and snap-on or clip-on feet.

Electronic

A machine described as 'electronic' will be a mechanical machine with electronic features. It must not be confused with computer machines, which are totally different.

The electronic features will be clearly listed by the manufacturer, and can cover such areas as the foot control, needle penetration and pattern selection.

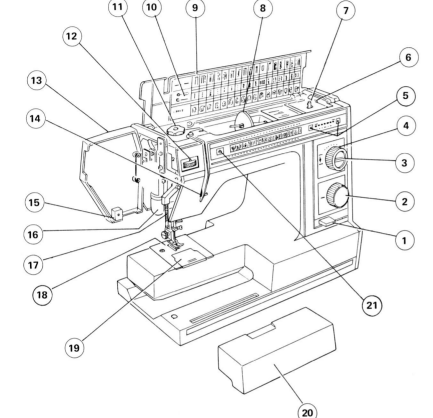

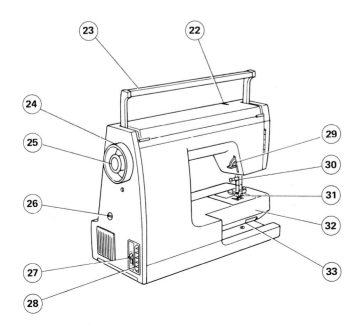

1	Reverse stitch lever
2	Pattern selector dial
3	Stitch length dial
4	Zigzag width dial
5	Speed level button
6	Bobbin winder stopper
7	Bobbin winder spindle
8	Spool holder (large)
9	Top cover
10	Flip-top sewing instruction panel
11	Pressure dial
12	Thread tension dial
13	Face plate
14	Check spring holder
15	Thread cutter
16	Sewing light
17	Needle threader
18	Needle plate
19	Slide plate
20	Extension table (Accessory storage box)
21	Up/Down needle position button
22	Thread take-up lever
23	Carrying handle
24	Balance wheel
25	Clutch knob
26	Feed balance dial
27	Power switch
28	Machine socket
29	Presser foot lifter
30	Needle clamp screw
31	Presser foot
32	Free arm
33	Drop feed lever

1.4 Example of a fully automatic free-arm

Computer

A computer machine will always include one or more microprocessors or 'chips' (Figure 1.5). It has far fewer moving parts than purely mechanical machines: all stitch selection, programming, buttonhole memorizing and so on is done by computer. The stitches and techniques will often be similar to those on electronic and automatic machines, but stitch selection is greatly simplified. There will also be stitch sequences and techniques not available with a normal mechanical machine.

In addition, these machines allow the user to store stitch and pattern data. Various patterns can be mixed together and adjusted to meet the requirements of the most dedicated sewer. On some models a totally original design can now be programmed into the machine using a variety of stitch co-ordinates.

Computer sewing is a specialist area, and for further reading and information refer to the author's *Complete Computer Sewing Book* (Heinemann, 1987). Despite the amazing range of these machines they can be the easiest to use and are recommended for beginner, dedicated sewer and professional alike.

When going out to purchase a new machine, take with you some notes on the type of stitches you want and the type of sewing you

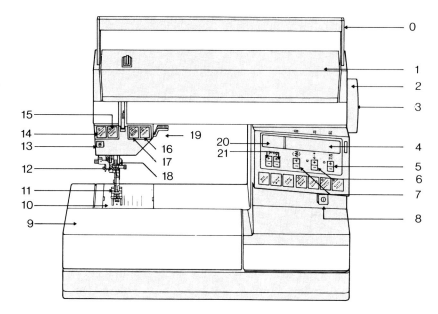

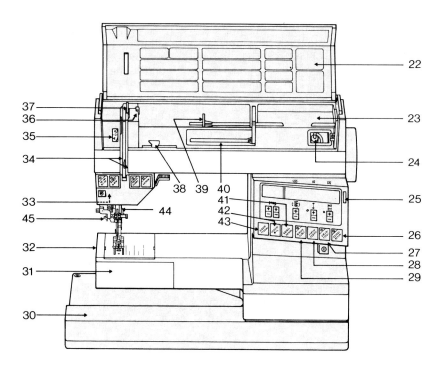

0 Carrying handle
1 Hinged top cover
2 Hand wheel
3 Stop motion knob
4 Display
5 Balancing-out & pattern length key
6 Stitch length & pattern length key
7 Stitch width key
8 Master switch
9 Detachable work support with accessory box and compartment
10 Needle plate
11 Sewing foot holder with sewing foot
12 Needle holder with set screw
13 Bobbin thread monitor light
14 "needle down" key
15 "sew slow" key
16 "reverse" key
17 "tie-off / buttonhole" key
18 Presser bar with thread cutter
19 Presser bar lifter
20 Program display
21 Programming keys (2)
22 Program chart (see sewing book)
23 Compartment for sewing data selector
24 Bobbin winder
25 Key for program cycle and sewing recommendations
26 "pattern mirroring" key
27 "single pattern" key
28 "pattern start" key
29 "twin needle" key
30 Base plate
31 Free arm cover, enclosing sewing hook
32 Free arm
33 Sewing light
34 Threading slots
35 Needle thread tension
36 Bobbin winder thread guide
37 Take-up lever
38 Bobbin winder thread guide (swing-out)
39 Spool holder with unreeling disc
40 Second spool holder (swing-up)
41 "repeat" key
42 "corrector" key
43 "program" key
44 Dual feed with thread cutter
45 Threader

1.5 Example of a computer machine

◆ BUYING YOUR MACHINE ◆

What the sewing machine needs to do	What the sewing machine needs to have
1 Simple skirts, tops, curtains, alterations, mending.	Straight stitch: zigzag. Tricot zigzag is an advantage. Clearly defined and easy to use controls. Light over the needle.
2 A lot of heavy work – tailoring, jeans, household items and upholstery.	A *heavy* machine incorporating the above. Set it in a sewing cabinet if you cannot move it easily, but remember that a lightweight machine in a cabinet will not have the same results.
3 Straightforward dressmaking in a variety of fabrics, some children's garments.	A free-arm machine: various needle positions: straight stitch: zigzag: tricot: straight stretch stitch: an *automatic* buttonhole: adjustable pressure on the presser foot: a good assortment of feet: colour-coded controls.
4 As 3 plus a lot of children's garments: a lot of fine fabrics: more advanced dressmaking.	As 3 but with a wider variety of stitches. Even if you do not use all the stitches you will have a machine that gives a better finish on the basic techniques. Also look out for outline zigzag for bulked fibres such as plushes and stretch towelling: overlocking: stretch overlocking: 7 mm needle swing (amazingly useful): feather stitch (very useful as well as decorative): basting: twin needle: snap-on feet: declutch bobbin winding.
5 Super, top-quality garments for yourself and family, with an individual touch: stylish accessories and/or craft items for the home.	You will certainly need all the things listed in 4. Invest in a really top-rate machine that does everything! A computerized machine will give you even more scope because you can program into it your own design interpretations. You will not use all 30+ stitches every time you sew, but it is wonderful to have everything you need built in for the occasion when you *do* need them.
6 Free embroidery.	All machines will do free embroidery, even elderly straight stitch models. If you are going to be very adventurous, go for the type with a bobbin case rather than a drop-in bobbin.
7 'I am a beginner – I want the simplest machine possible!'	If you can afford it then go for the computerized machine too! It really is the simplest machine to use because it does the thinking for you, and it takes all the worry out of having to set the dials for various stitch lengths and widths. If you cannot afford the computer machine then have a good colour-coded system.

are going to do (crafts, household, dressmaking and so on: see table). Take some fabric samples too. Always ask to use the machine yourself; do not rely on just looking. Machines can handle very differently, and you must feel at home with the foot control and the knobs, dials or buttons on the facia for stitch selection and stitch width and length control. It is important that you can sew very slowly by controlling the foot pedal. Many machines have *exact* one-stitch-at-a-time control, so if the one you are testing tends to run away with you just move on to a different model. Look closely at the stitch formations and sequences and ensure quality stitching. My test for a machine is superb, smooth and exact satin stitching: if the machine performs this well, everything else will probably be excellent too.

LEARNING ABOUT THE MACHINE

◆ CONTROL

Master the control you have over the machine. Plug the machine into the mains, switch it on, but do *not* thread it. Now keep starting and stopping it to get used to the foot pedal. Machines with electronic or computer features will have instant, perfect stitch-by-stitch control, but you need to learn just how hard to press on the foot pedal to obtain this. With more basic models, you may hear a buzzing noise when you touch the pedal; if so, just push a little harder and perhaps slightly turn the balance wheel to get started. Learning to control the machine with the foot pedal is just like learning to drive a car and master the gears.

One machine on the market (Jones & Brother *Opus*) can be controlled totally with hand buttons as well as with a foot pedal; these hand controls can be mastered in the same way.

◆ THREADING

Learn how to thread the machine (Figure 1.6). With reference to the manufacturer's handbook, slowly thread the top system. Keep threading up and unthreading until you are able to do it quickly and easily. If you follow the correct route it is difficult to mis-thread an easy-thread system. On a machine that has an obvious tension unit *outside* the machine casing, take great care to pass the thread *between* the silver discs in the tension unit; if your thread slips outside these discs, the machine will not sew.

When you understand the threading of the top system, refer to the instruction book again and then

7

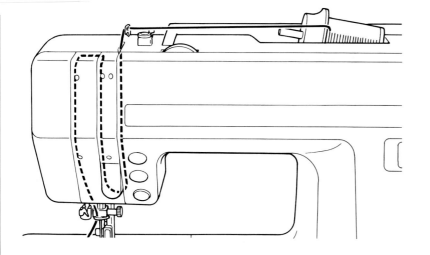

1.6 Example of an easy-thread system

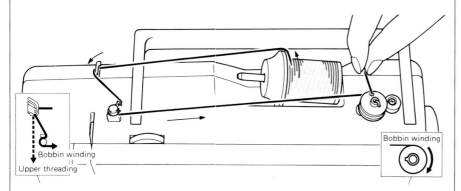

1.7 Example of bobbin winding

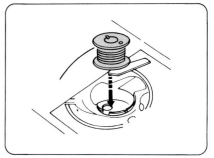

Place the bobbin in the bobbin holder with the thread running counter-clockwise.

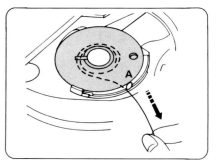

Guide the thread into notch A on the front side of the bobbin holder. Draw the thread to the left, sliding it between the tension spring blades.

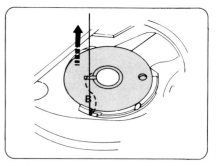

Continue to draw lightly on the thread until the thread slips into notch B.

1.8 Example of a drop-in bobbin

wind and thread the bobbin (Figure 1.7). There are two types of bobbin: the drop-in bobbin, and the type that goes first into a bobbin case before being inserted into the machine. A drop-in bobbin is inserted into the machine just under the needle on the top of the free arm (Figure 1.8). The bobbin case will be inserted from the front or side of the machine (Figure 1.9). The part into which the bobbin fits is called the raceway. Here again there are two different systems: one has a full rotary hook, and the other an oscillating hook. The full rotary hook is normally smooth running and jam-proof, and it can be either drop-in or the front-loading bobbin case. Whichever method you have, ensure that the bobbin thread is passed correctly through the tension spring or the machine will not stitch correctly.

◆ STITCHING

Start to practise stitching on a firm piece of cloth, such as sheeting. Stitch practice lengths of every stitch your machine will perform, on every width and length setting. Note the differences, and if necessary make notes directly on to your practice cloth with a felt-tip pen to help you remember what the settings were. Remember that variations of width and length will often make a stitch look totally different (Figures 1.10 and 1.11). For example, a feather stitch on a width of 7 will look very different from a feather stitch on a width of 3. Again, a satin stitch pattern will look very different when the stitch length is set longer and the pattern is opened out.

When you have tried, tested and experimented with all the stitches, use the different presser feet to try out the techniques of hemming, buttonholing, overedging and so on.

When you are confident about using the controls, dip into your bag of offcuts and try the various stitches and techniques on different fabrics. Notice that many stitches look and perform differently on a variety of fabrics because of the weight of cloth, the firmness of weave or other factors. Do *not* expect the stitches to look exactly the same on a fine voile and a heavy coating: the stitching is not wrong, just different.

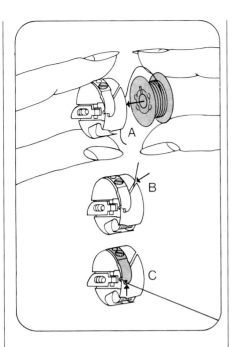

Insert bobbin so that thread unwinds towards the back (A). Draw the thread into slot B and into eye C.

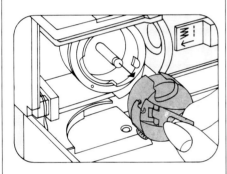

Inserting the bobbin case into the machine.

1.9 Example of bobbin and bobbin case.

◆ **EXPERIMENTING**

Allow time to 'play' with your machine all through its working life! Try not to get the machine out only when you have a serious sewing task; if you find some spare time,

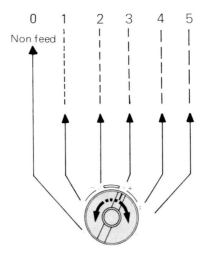

1.10 Adjusting stitch length

have fun experimenting. In this way you will constantly learn and benefit from your primary piece of sewing equipment.

◆ **DOS AND DON'TS**

Do:

1 Use your machine on a firm table and at a comfortable height.

2 Sit on a comfortable chair at a suitable height for the table you use.

3 Make sure there is adequate lighting.

4 Keep the machine clean and dust-free. Cover when not in use.

5 Thread slowly and carefully. If the machine does not stitch perfectly, take out the thread and start again. It is a fact that most problems with a machine stem from mis-threading.

6 Make sure that the needle is inserted the correct way round. The machine will not stitch if the needle is inserted back to front.

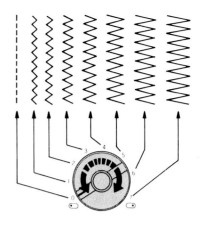

1.11 Adjusting stitch width

7 Always pull the work out from the machine away from you; this takes strain off the needle.

8 Set the needle at the highest position when you pull out the work. The most modern machines automatically stop with the needle up; with other machines you must raise the needle with the balance wheel, if necessary, before pulling the work out.

9 Hold on to the ends of threads when you start to stitch, just to make sure they do not slip down inside the raceway and jam the machine.

Don't:

1 Twiddle with the tension knob or dial. A well set-up machine will stitch 90 per cent of your sewing *without* adjustment. If a stitch appears mis-formed, try adjusting the stitch width *before* altering the tension.

2 Tackle a big new venture before experimenting thoroughly with your new machine.

BASIC STITCHES AND TECHNIQUES

Stitches and techniques are dealt with fully in Part 5, but some basic principles are given here.

There are still some straight stitch machines in use, but these days most sewers want zigzag at the very least. A swing needle machine is just a machine that will do zigzag, so *any* machine other than a straight stitch machine is a swing needle model. The minimum swing on a machine will be 5 mm, but many models now go to 7 mm or even 8 mm. Every machine will be fully adjustable within its own width of swing.

The stitch length now varies considerably – from the tiniest stitch to 12 mm or more!

Most sewers who wish to tackle basic fashion or sewing for the home will easily use a range of 6–8 stitches (Figure 1.12). This will provide for stretch and overedge work and buttonholes – that is, utility stitching but not necessarily decorative

work (Figures 1.13 and 1.14). Your interest and enthusiasm will dictate how much more you want. Once you are used to a machine, you may regret that you did not buy a better model to give even more scope. *Always* purchase the very best

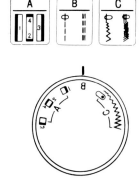

1.12 Stitches and selector dial on a basic machine. This model will do a four-step buttonhole and straight, straight stretch, zigzag and stretch zigzag stitches

machine you can afford, and grow into it! If you require exceptionally good stitch performance you must buy from the top of the range; like any other modern product, you get what you pay for.

◆ STITCHES

A *stitch* is either a row of straight stitches, a zigzag, or a more complicated pattern of utility or decorative use.

◆ TECHNIQUES

A *technique* is something that you do with the stitch – quilting, zip insertion, top stitching, buttonholes and so on.

A selection of *presser feet* is supplied with the machine to enable special techniques to be performed well (Figure 1.15). They have all sorts of slits, bars, prongs, grooves and spirals etc., and may be metal

Pattern	⊕	⊕	Mmm	⋮⋮⋮	⋀⋀	⋁	⋁	▯⊞▮	⊕	⊕	Mmm	⋀⋀⋀	⋀	⊨
Stitch length dial	1.5 ~ 4		0.3 ~ 4	0.5 ~ 1.5	1 ~ 3		0.5 ~ 1.5	0.3 ~ 1	S.S.					
Stitch	¦	¦	⋛	⋛	⋀⋀	⋁⋁	⋁⋁	⋛	❘	❘	⋀⋀	⋀⋀⋀	⋀⋀	⊨

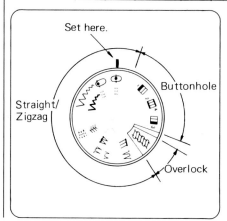

1.13 Stitches and selector dial on a machine that provides a good range of utility stitches and a buttonhole. This model will do overcasting, blind hemming, feather and tricot stitches as well as straight, straight stretch and zigzag stitches

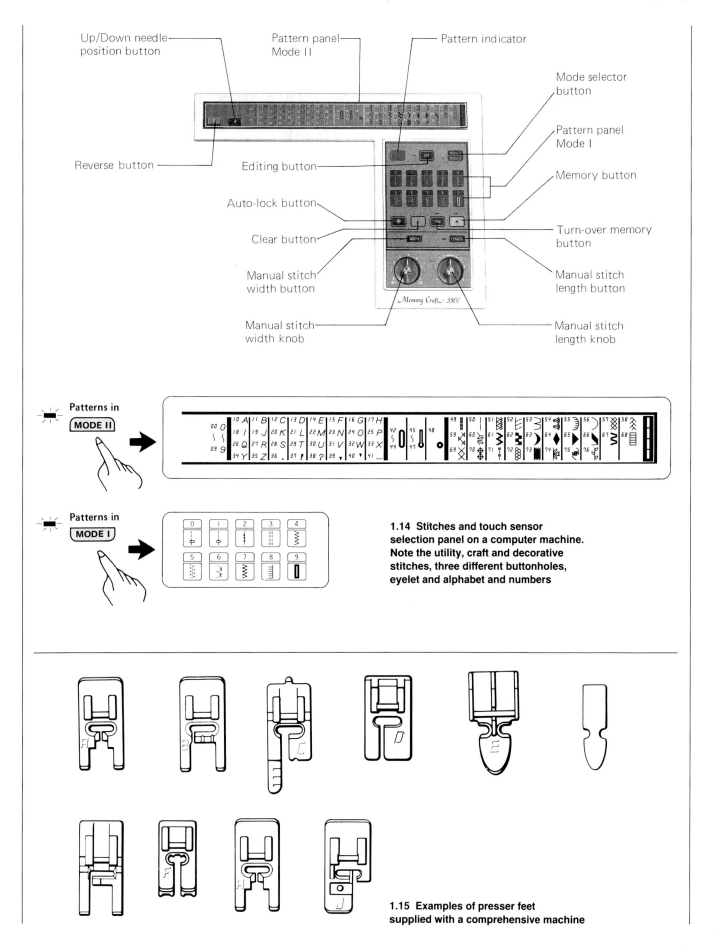

Up/Down needle position button

Pattern panel Mode II

Pattern indicator

Mode selector button

Pattern panel Mode I

Memory button

Reverse button

Editing button

Auto-lock button

Clear button

Turn-over memory button

Manual stitch width button

Manual stitch length button

Manual stitch width knob

Manual stitch length knob

Memory Craft 5500

Patterns in **MODE II**

Patterns in **MODE I**

1.14 **Stitches and touch sensor selection panel on a computer machine. Note the utility, craft and decorative stitches, three different buttonholes, eyelet and alphabet and numbers**

1.15 **Examples of presser feet supplied with a comprehensive machine**

1.16 Clip-on feet (Bernina)

1.17 Sewing jeans (Elna)

or plastic. Clear plastic feet are usually used when you need to see what is being stitched immediately under the foot, such as embroidery or buttonholes; they are usually strengthened with metal shanks. Most modern feet clip easily and quickly on and off the presser foot holder, which in turn is screwed on to the presser foot bar in the usual way (Figure 1.16).

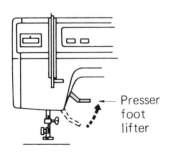

1.18 Presser foot lever under the arch of the machine

It is becoming more and more common to find the presser foot lever placed to the right of the needle bar *under* the arch of the machine instead of at the back (Figure 1.18). Once the machine operator gets used to this position it will be found very comfortable.

◆ IMPORTANT FEATURES ON A MACHINE

The following features are those that I feel are important to consider when purchasing a new machine (Figure 1.19). The type of sewing – fashion, crafts, toys, sewing for the home, stitching very light fabrics or very heavy fabrics and leathers, and so on – must also be taken into consideration. It is a good idea to list what you require from a machine before you examine what is on the market.

◇ *Free arm* For sleeves, cuffs, armholes, trouser legs, necks, children's wear, toys, dolls and all intricate areas.

◇ *Ease of stitch selection/programming* Clear, simple dials and controls and a well-written manufacturer's handbook are vital.

◇ *Number of stitches* You need a good selection of stitches for the type of work you intend to do.

◇ *Number of memories* When purchasing a computer machine, ensure there are adequate memory facilities.

◇ *Needle positions* Most important! Ensure that the needle can be moved to variable positions for straight stitching, stretch stitching, top stitching and so on.

◇ *Needle stop up/down* It is a tremendous help if the needle always stops in the highest 'up' position. Some machines have a 'down' stop facility: this is useful if you are doing a lot of embroidery, appliqué, top stitching and so on, where you need to have the needle in the fabric, raise the presser foot and reposition the fabric before continuing to stitch.

◇ *Auto lock off* A simple function but most useful for very fine work, embroidery and motif sewing.

◇ *Buttonholes* Automatic buttonholes are an absolute *must*. Some machines have adjustment on the width of the buttonhole, so that you can make a very narrow one on fine fabrics, lingerie and babywear and a wide one on suits and coats. Computer machines will usually have a selection of up to five different types, such as square ends, rounded ends, one square and one rounded, keyhole, and double stitched. There are a number of different systems for performing buttonholes on automatic, electronic and computer machines; it is advisable to compare the methods on the machines before purchase as they do vary considerably.

◇ *Easy-thread system* A quick and easy one-hand threading system saving time and problems.

◇ *Full rotary hook* This will ensure smooth and (usually) jam-proof sewing.

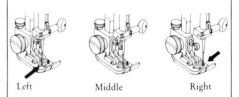

Left   Middle   Right

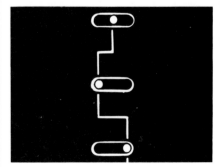

1.19 Variable needle positions

◇ *Needle penetration* Machines with electronic features and computer machines will often have exceptional needle penetration, slicing through many layers of heavy fabric as easily as one layer of voile! (Figure 1.17.)
◇ *Foot pedal and machine control* Try the machine in the shop to make sure that the foot pedal is comfortable for the size of *your* foot. It is often more comfortable to use the pedal bare-footed. Ensure that the machine responds to stitch-by-stitch control with the foot pedal.
◇ *Accessories stowed in the machine* Accessories stowed within the machine head (lift-up lid) or in a box attached to the machine (remov-able to expose the free arm) elimin-ate the problems of misplacement.
◇ *Retractable leads* These are sur-prisingly convenient!
◇ *Weight* This is very important! A machine has to be moved around the house and lifted on and off tables. It must not be too heavy for the operator to carry comfortably.

SPECIAL FEATURES AND ATTACHMENTS

Many machines, have special attach-ments, either supplied with them or obtainable from the manufacturers as optional extras. I list a number of these items here.

It should be noted that whilst some items are interchangeable be-tween models, others will fit only one make or model of machine.

◆ CUT 'N' SEW
(*Bernina*)

◆ SIDE CUTTER
(*Brother and New Home*)

These two attachments are similar and perform the same task – to trim the fabric (similar to an overlocker) whilst the overedge stitching is being performed. Figure 1.20 shows the cut 'n' sew attached to the Ber-nina 1130 and Figure 1.21 shows in diagram form the side cutter on the Brother Compal Opus.

1.20 Cut 'n' Sew on Bernina 1130
(Bernina)

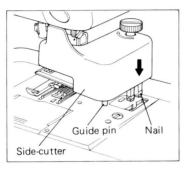

Fitting the cutter: locate the guide pin above the hole and insert the nail into the machine.

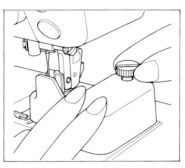

Fasten the screw.

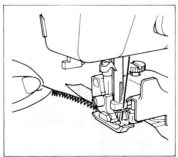

Both threads are passed through the lower side of the presser foot and held lightly with the fingers. The fabric is trimmed as it is stitched. Adjust the stitch width according to the fabric.

1.21 Side cutter on Brother *Compal Opus*

1.22 Side cutter on Brother *Compal Opus* (Jones & Brother)

◆ WALKING FOOT
(*Bernina, Riccar, Singer*)

This foot performs the same func-tion as dual feed (Figure 1.23). It is fitted to the machine in the normal way. (Note: this is an optional extra and must be purchased separately.)

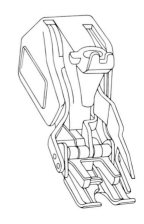

1.23 Walking foot

◆ PATCHING AND MENDING FOOT
(*Singer*)

In appearance this is similar to the walking foot. It is attached in the same way and is controlled by a lever around the needle bar. A preprogrammed stitch sequence in the machine controls the needle movements: direction stitching is therefore easily obtained (Figures 1.24, 1.25 and 1.26).

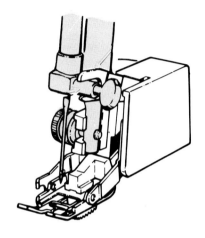

1.24 Patching and mending foot (Singer)

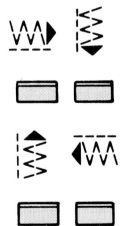

1.25 Four directional controls for patching (Singer)

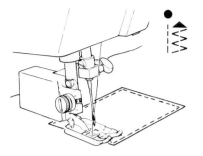

(a) Stitching around the patch with straight stitch.

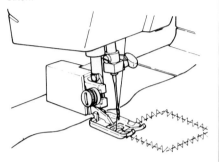

(b) The patch is then secured with zigzag or tricot stitch.

1.26 Two stages within the patching sequence (Singer)

◆ KNEE LIFT
(*Bernina*)

When fitted a touch on the bar with the knee will raise or lower the presser foot (Figure 1.27). This is useful when you require both hands to move the work during embroidery or other detailed stitching.

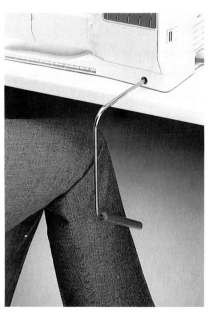

1.27 Knee lift on Bernina 1130 (Bernina)

◆ DUAL FEED
(*Pfaff*)

Dual feed is exclusive to Pfaff (Figure 1.28). It solves the problem of fabrics moving on each other during sewing, both by holding the fabric firmly and by feeding the fabrics from above and below simultaneously.

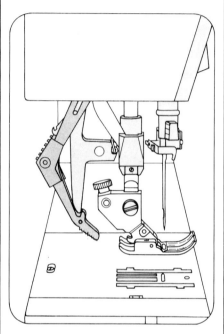

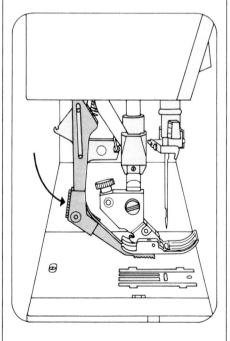

1.28 Dual feed: to engage, lower the top feed until it snaps into place

◆ ROLLER FOOT

Most companies make a roller foot to either screw or clip on to the machine (Figure 1.29). It is a very inexpensive and easy way to cope with slippery fabrics, piles, fur fabrics, leathers, PVC and so on.

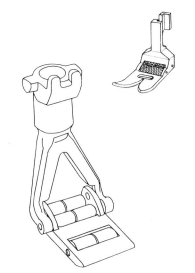

Roller feet

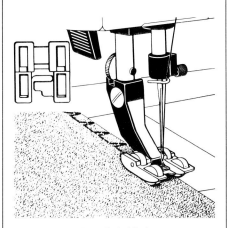

Roller presser foot. Suitable for coarse-knitted material, certain knit and stretch fabrics, as well as leather imitations and plastic material.

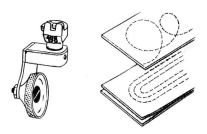

Foot with roller for leather.

1.29 Samples of various roller feet

◆ BLIND HEM FOOT
(*all makes*)

Every make of machine has a blind hem foot, usually supplied with the machine (Figure 1.30). In recent years these feet have been considerably improved in design, and updating is recommended; they can be purchased as an optional extra.

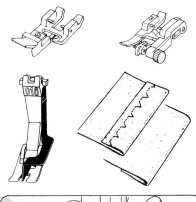

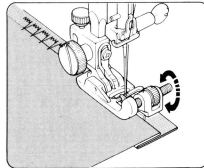

1.30 Blind hem feet

◆ FELL or LAP SEAM FOOT

This small foot makes such seaming easier (Figure 1.31). Useful for jeans etc. where this type of seam is required.

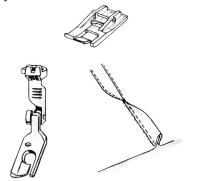

1.31 Fell or lap seam foot

◆ ELASTIC GATHERER
(*Elna*)

This little gadget is very efficient, and is suitable in particular for lingerie (Figure 1.32).

An elastic gathering foot is also an optional extra with some overlockers: the working principle is similar, and the end result is the same.

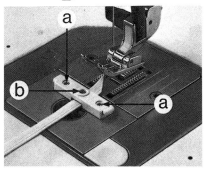

1.32 Gatherer for elastic: for gathering lingerie fabrics and fabrics of medium thickness. Use elastic that is 4–6 mm wide. It is stretched automatically while sewing.

◆ BUTTON SEWING FOOT
(most makes)

By dropping the feed, setting the machine to zigzag and aligning the holes of the button with the slot in the foot, a well-stitched on button is obtained (Figure 1.33). Adjust the zigzag to the width of the holes.

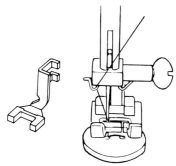

1.33 Button sewing foot

◆ BUTTONHOLE FOOT
(all makes)

The buttonhole foot is supplied with all makes, but some special types are available with some models or as an optional extra. Illustrated are some special feet.

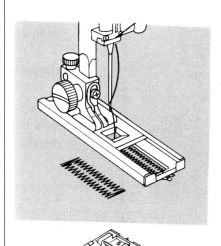

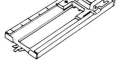

1.34 Slider feet

The Bernina foot with a magic eye is supplied with their computer models (Figure 1.37). This measures the length of the first side, and ensures that the second side is exactly equal. The New Home *Memory Craft 7000* has a similar presser foot.

Slider feet are also popular now, and make corded buttonholes easy (Figure 1.34). They can be purchased to fit most machines.

On some models, special feet are available which hold the button whilst the machine is sewing the buttonhole to the button size (Figure 1.35).

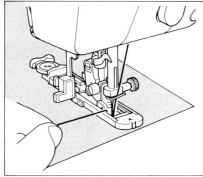

1.35 Slider foot which holds the button

◆ BUTTONHOLE CUTTER
(all makes)

All machines come complete with this handy gadget (Figure 1.36). Use it for cutting buttonholes cleanly and accurately as shown.

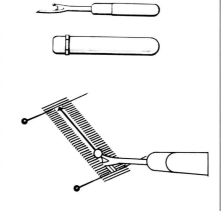

1.36 Cutting open buttonholes

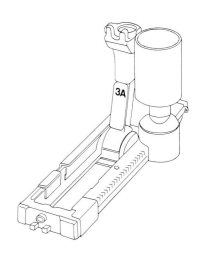

1.37 Bernina 'magic eye'

◆ ZIPPER/PIPING FOOT
(all makes)

All machines come supplied with a zipper foot; this foot is also used for piping.

A screw-on foot has been supplied for many years (Figure 1.38). Newer models can have much smaller and neater clip-on feet. New Home and Pfaff supply a special zipper foot for inserting invisible zippers, or offer it as an optional extra (see instructions in Part 5).

A few of the new clip-on feet are not suitable for piping as the needle cannot get right under the piping cord if it is a large and bulky one; if you have problems, purchase a screw-on foot.

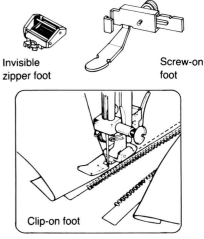

Invisible zipper foot

Screw-on foot

Clip-on foot

1.38 Zipper feet

◆ QUILTING/EDGING GUIDE
(*all makes*)

This is normally supplied with the machine (Figure 1.49). I mention it here because, whilst many people know of its use for quilting, surprisingly few use it as an aid to edge sewing. For edge stitching further from the edge of the garment than 12 mm, or for decorative borders, this guide is equally useful.

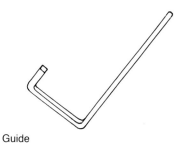

Guide

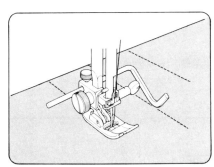

Quilting

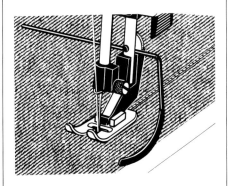

Edgestitching

1.39 Quilting/edging guide

◆ FAGGOTTING PLATE
(*Elna*)

This is a simple little guide which fits on to the hook cover and guides the two pieces of fabric through the needle area with exactly the right space between them (Figure 1.40).

1.40 Faggotting plate

◆ TAILOR TACK/ FRINGE FOOT
(*Bernina, Elna, Pfaff, Viking*)

By sewing over the centre prong, a row of loops is formed (Figure 1.41). This can be used for tailor tacks and various forms of decorative sewing.

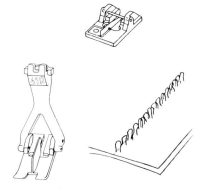

1.41 Tailor tack foot

◆ CORDING FOOT
(*most makes*)

Cording feet are for applying or couching fine cords or threads in a decorative manner (Figure 1.42) The cords are threaded through the holes in the foot and then under the foot. Whichever direction the pattern is sewn, the cords will follow the line of stitching.

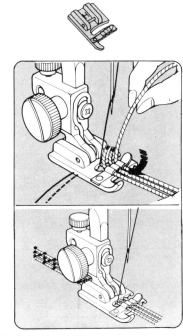

Cords held in a clip

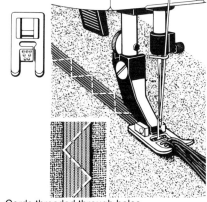

Cords threaded through holes

1.42 Different cording feet

◆ PIN TUCK/ CORDING FOOT

This grooved foot is for machine pin tucks (see Part 5). The pin tucks are stitched with a twin needle and are very fine (Figure 1.43). A cord can be inserted *under* the fabric and enclosed in the tuck for a more ridged effect.

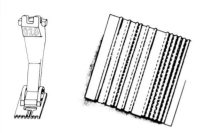

1.43 Pin tuck foot

◆ BINDER
(*most makes*)

This accessory is still freely available as an optional extra to fit most models of machine. A screw-on shank will fit most machines, but clip-on binders can now be obtained. Figure 1.44 shows illustrations from Bernina and Viking. The binder is a quick and efficient way of applying a binding to fashion, crafts or household items.

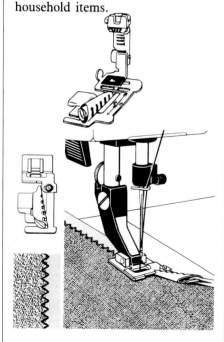

1.44 Binder

◆ RUFFLER
(*most makes*)

This is another optional extra available for most machines, which – like the binder – many think is now obsolete! The ruffler can be adjusted to provide small tucks of exactly equal measurement, and is most efficient for stitching bed covers, drapes and so on where particularly long flounces are required. The size of tucks can be easily adjusted, and this is not such a fearsome attachment as it looks! (Figure 1.45.)

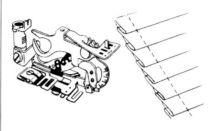

1.45 Ruffler

◆ EYELET
(*Viking, Pfaff*)

This small attachment is fitted to the base plate (Figure 1.46). A hole is made in the cloth or belt and fitted over the little knob; the machine then neatly finishes off the raw edge. (Note: many computer machines of all makes will do a pre-programmed eyelet too.)

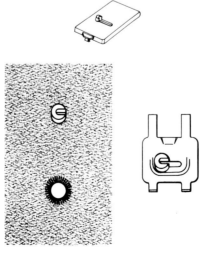

1.46 Eyelet stitcher

◆ HEM STITCHER
(*Viking*)

Place the fork between two layers of fabric and sew together with long straight stitches for a neat hem stitch line (Figure 1.47).

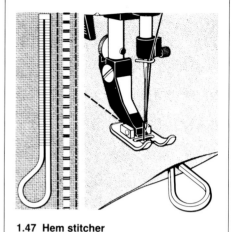

1.47 Hem stitcher

◆ ENGLISH EMBROIDERY ATTACHMENT
(*Bernina*)

Often called Broderie Anglaise, English embroidery is attractive for lingerie, children's wear, babywear and delicate summer clothes. Full instructions are supplied with the kit, which is an optional extra for selected Bernina models (Figure 1.48).

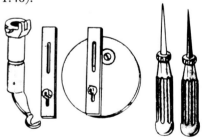

1.48 English embroidery attachment

◆ WEAVER'S REED
(*Viking*)

Reeds come in two widths for rug sewing (Figure 1.49). Wind the yarn over the reed and sew in place with straight stitch. The reed is an optional extra.

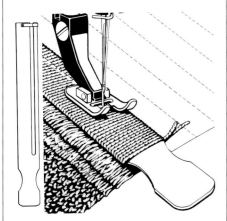

1.49 Weaver's reed

◆ GATHERING FOOT
(*most makes*)

This is normally an optional extra (Figure 1.39). It is worth purchasing if you do an exceptional amount of gathering, such as on bed frills, cushion frills and fashion items for bridal and evening wear.

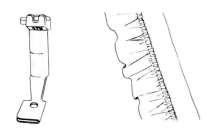

1.50 Gathering foot

◆ CIRCULAR EMBROIDERY ATTACHMENT
(*Bernina*)

This is a simple device which enables programmed embroidery stitches to be sewn in a true circle (Figure 1.52). It is an optional extra.

◆ EMBROIDERY/ DARNING FOOT
(*most makes*)

With various fittings for the machine, these feet all make free darning and embroidery a simple task (Figure 1.51). You can move the fabric freely underneath the foot but each time the needle is down in the fabric the embroidery foot will also be down, thus holding the fabric whilst the stitch is formed – unlike true free embroidery, where no foot is used at all. If you find free embroidery extremely difficult – try this!

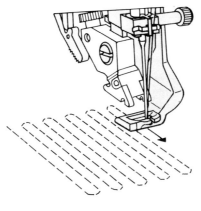

1.51 Embroidery/darning foot

1.52 Circular embroidery attachment

◆ CIRCULAR SEWING PIVOT
(*Elna*)

This is another simple device for circular sewing (Figure 1.53). The pivot is placed through the fabric into one of the holes on the extension plate. The distance from the pivot to the needle is the radius of the circle sewn.

Pivot

Pivot in position

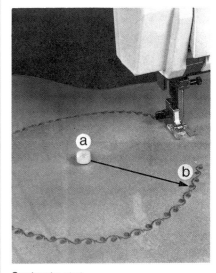

Sewing the circle

1.53 Circular sewing

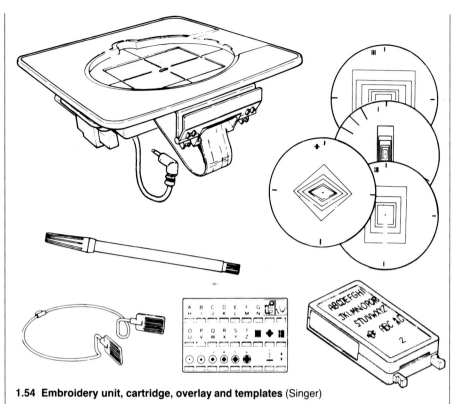

1.54 Embroidery unit, cartridge, overlay and templates (Singer)

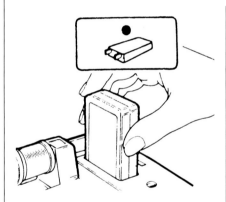

1.55 Inserting the cartridge (Singer)

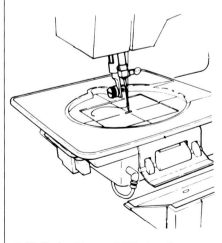

1.56 Embroidery unit fitted on the machine (Singer)

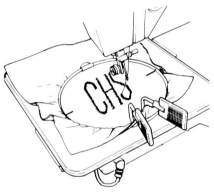

1.57 Monogram stitiching (Singer)

1.58 Style of monogram: line, diamond, block (Singer)

◆ SEW WARE CARTRIDGES
(*Singer*)

These cartridges contain alphabets, numbers, large monograms and various motif patterns. The cartridges are inserted into the machine and complemented with an overlay panel to slot on to the machine facia (Figures 1.54 to 1.58). When the machine is programmed, the embroidery unit performs the required function. The embroidery unit comes complete with cassettes, overlay, four clear placement templates and a vanishing marker pencil. Some cartridges come with the Singer *Symphonie 300*, and others can be purchased as an optional extra.

◆ EMBROIDERY FRAMES/HOOPS
(*various makes*)

Frames (or hoops) come in various sizes, with either a screw fitting or spring clip (Figure 1.59). The fabric is held tautly between the two circles. Use the frame for free embroidery or free darning. It is purchased as an optional extra.

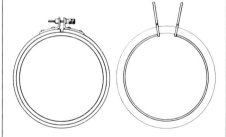

1.59 Two types of embroidery frame or hoop

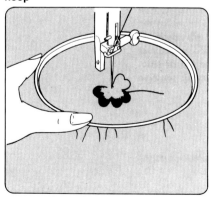

1.60 The frame in use.

CHERISHING YOUR MACHINE

All machines should be loved and cherished. Establish a good working relationship with your machine; understand its systems and programs; do lots of experimenting and note your findings; discover its foibles and its strengths; discover its reactions on various fabrics; and so on.

You should have many years of happy sewing with care and one or two basic maintenance checks, provided you remember that you are dealing with precision equipment.

Thread both bobbin and upper thread systems carefully. Misthreading accounts for a large number of problems. Thread and rethread over and over again when you first get the machine, until it is instinctive: however, always thread through the system slowly even when you are well acquainted with the machine, just to be *sure*! Even with easy-thread systems, over-haste still causes the occasional mishap.

Change needles frequently; a blunt needle causes problems. Clean the machine often. Modern fabrics and thread do lint or fluff a lot, and it is very important that this does not build up in and around the moving parts. Reference to your manufacturer's manual will show how to remove raceway and needle plate to facilitate cleaning around this area (Figure 1.61). It is necessary to remove the needle plate to get to the feed dog; if enough fluff accumulates here, it will eventually pack down hard and stop the feed dog moving. Brush around the needle clamp area too.

Most modern machines do not normally require oiling. However,

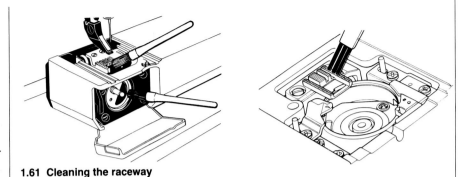

1.61 Cleaning the raceway

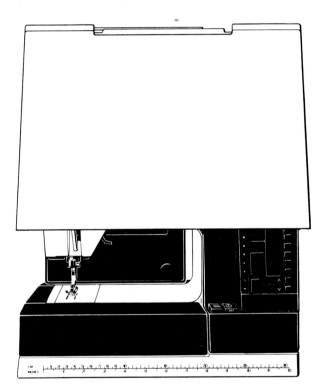

1.62 Cover machine when not in use

the manufacturer's handbook will explain where to oil if it is necessary.

Do remember to keep the machine head casing clean too. Wipe over it with a soft cloth; avoid strong cleaners and detergents.

A quick check and clean at the end of each project will increase the life of the machine. Keep it covered with its dust cover or lid when not in use, and store away from heat, damp or direct sunshine (Figure 1.62).

OVERLOCKERS

It is not always appreciated what a boon these machines are to the busy sewer, and to what extent they complement the normal domestic sewing machine. Overlockers are often promoted as a machine to take the place of the normal machine, but unless you are totally into sportswear and T-shirt dressing then the overlocker must go hand-in-hand with an ordinary machine!

The main benefits of an overlocker are:

◇ Speed.
◇ Professional (industrial) stitch sequence.
◇ Ability to sew with wool, bulked thread, and quite thick decorative threads.
◇ Cut/trim and overstitch edges in one operation.

Other benefits include:

◇ Exceptional rolled edges.
◇ Quick and easy flat-lock seams.
◇ Proficient blind hemming.
◇ Decorative craft finishes.

There are a wide variety of overlockers now available, taking from two to five threads and performing a variety of different tasks. Some machines will only stitch with the required number of threads, whilst others will convert from say four to three. Machines being produced now normally have differential feed for extra control.

These little machines have come on to the domestic scene from the professional workroom and small factory unit. The first ones were very utilitarian in appearance, and many adjustments had to be made with a screwdriver or spanner. The latest overlockers are as streamlined as their domestic sewing machine cousins, with easy adjustment by appropriate dials.

With their suspended threads, multiple tension units and twin needles, overlockers look complicated. However, they always have colour-coded thread charts on their casings. The simple way to get to grips with this type of stitching is to thread the machines with the appropriate colour-matching thread, so that you can see easily what thread makes what part of the sequence and what the results of tension adjustments are. After this initial exercise the machine will be less intimidating.

Check that there is a light over the needle – earlier models did not have this feature – and also check the type of needles required. Some of the overlockers use normal domestic sewing machine needles, whilst others require a special type: all are freely available from the stores and dealers selling the specific models. The machines will all take very large cops of thread, which is important because they eat it at a tremendous rate! A trick when rethreading with a new colour is not to pull out all the threads and then start again, but to snip the cottons by the overhead suspension guides and knot them on to the new cops. Run the machine, and the looper threads will easily come right through – knots and all! The needle threads will pass through the system at least as far as the eye of the needles; this will save much time.

1.63 Rolled edges are a wonderful way to edge frills: quick and easy on an overlocker (McCabe)

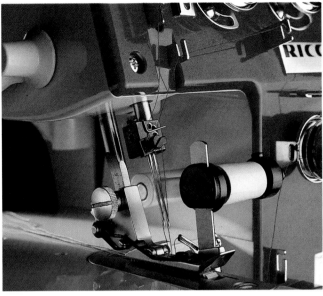

(a) Needle threads and a looper thread.

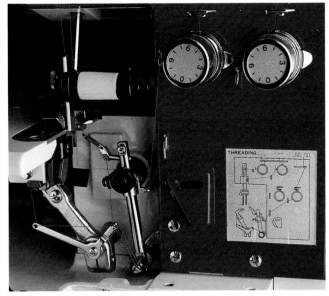

(b) Looper threads and threading colour coding.

1.64 Overlocker details (Riccar)

Cutting and overlocking.

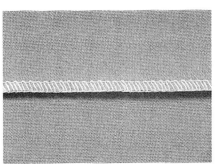

Sewing together, cutting and overlocking.

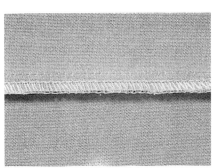

With safety double-chain stitch.

With central safety stitch designed for elastic materials and knitted fabrics.

Overlocking cross seams.

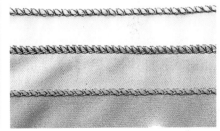

A beautiful rolled or narrow hem is easily achieved on fine fabrics.

1.65 The most useful overlocker stitch sequences (Riccar)

There are no bobbins on over-lockers; instead, loopers make the overedge (binding) part of the stitch sequence. Thus all the threads are 'top' threads, and this is why there are tension units for each thread in use. There will be permutations of needle threads and looper threads according to the number of threads in use.

1.66 Special differential feed mechanism on some models virtually eliminates puckering on highly stretchable fabrics and knitted woollens (Riccar)

23

◆ THE NEW HOME *COMBI DX*

This machine is unique because it combines the features and stitches of a domestic sewing machine with the facilities of a two-thread over-locker – on the other end of the machine! When the overlock stitch is required, a simple flick of a switch brings the other end into use. The turntable makes it very easy to swivel the machine around.

The stitches incorporated are the basic dressmaking stitches – straight, zigzag, stretch and blind hem stitches, buttonholes, and so on. The two-thread overlock stitch will neaten whilst the cutter trims the edges of the seam allowance. The stitch quality is good, and this is an ideal machine for beginners or for dedicated sewers with limited space.

1.67 New Home *Combi DX:* the normal sewing machine at the front

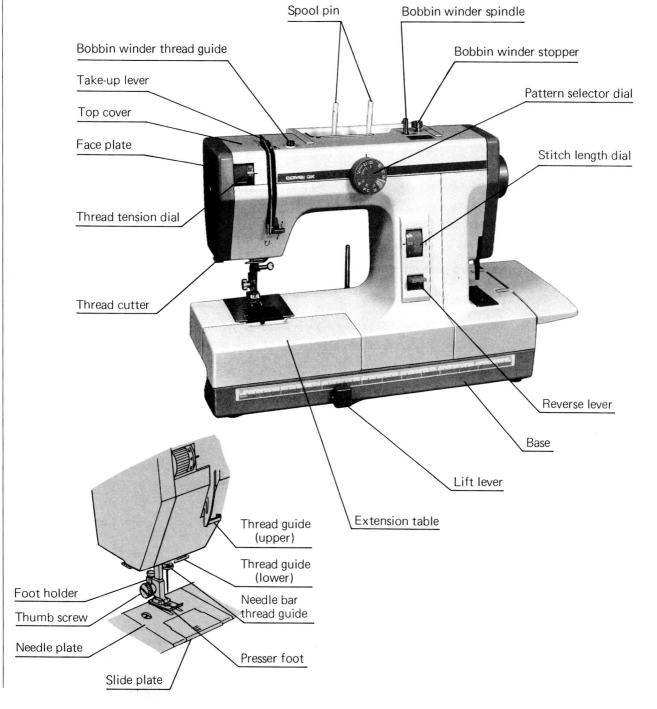

Spool pin

Bobbin winder spindle

Bobbin winder thread guide

Bobbin winder stopper

Take-up lever

Pattern selector dial

Top cover

Face plate

Stitch length dial

Thread tension dial

Thread cutter

Reverse lever

Base

Lift lever

Extension table

Thread guide (upper)

Thread guide (lower)

Foot holder

Needle bar thread guide

Thumb screw

Needle plate

Presser foot

Slide plate

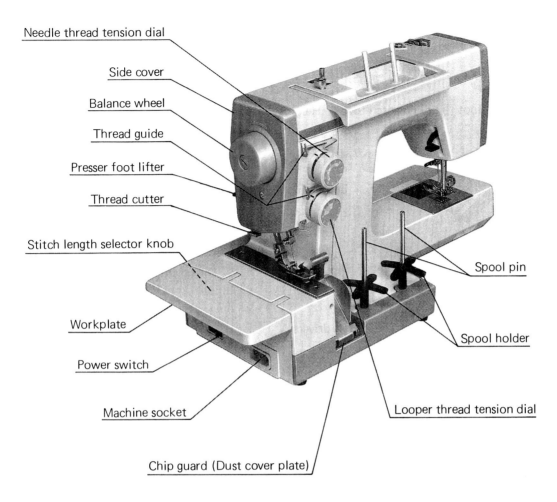

Needle thread tension dial

Side cover

Balance wheel

Thread guide

Presser foot lifter

Thread cutter

Stitch length selector knob

Workplate

Power switch

Machine socket

Spool pin

Spool holder

Looper thread tension dial

Chip guard (Dust cover plate)

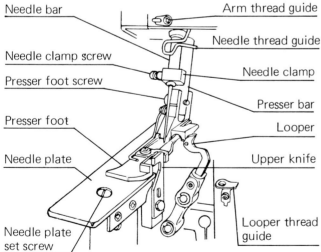

Needle bar

Needle clamp screw

Presser foot screw

Presser foot

Needle plate

Needle plate set screw

Arm thread guide

Needle thread guide

Needle clamp

Presser bar

Looper

Upper knife

Looper thread guide

1.68 New Home *Combi DX:* two thread overlocker at the back

25

2 · FABRICS

CHOOSING FABRICS

Whatever you are sewing, fabric is the most important ingredient. Always choose the best quality that you can afford for the job in hand: good quality fabric will give a better finish and stand up better to wear and tear. When you are experienced with fabrics it is possible to raid markets and sales for bargains, but until then go to a reputable retailer where you can get help and advice if you need it.

When choosing fabrics there are a number of basic things to take into account:

◇ Fibre content
◇ Colour
◇ Pattern/plain
◇ Texture
◇ Warmth/coolness
◇ Stiffness/drapability
◇ Durability
◇ Cleaning and wash codes.

Many fabricoholics gather up fabrics because of eye appeal at every opportunity and store them until they have the chance to use them. The amount to buy in this instance comes with experience. When you are starting to sew, fabric purchasing goes hand in hand with pattern buying: the pattern envelope will advise on suitable fabrics for the style illustrated and will give the yardage required (see Chapter 3). In crafts and household sewing the fabric choice is equally important. Always make sure the material is equal to the job in hand. Flimsy fabrics may look fine, but for loose covers would be totally impractical – or that heavy brocade may be too stiff for drapes! If in doubt, seek expert guidance from the salesperson.

Fibre content is important. Natural, man-made or a mixture of these fibres will all have different characteristics: wool is warm, cotton is cool, and so on. Whatever the yarns, whether they are woven or knitted will also affect the durability and hang of the fabric: so too will the different *types* of weaves and knits. Look for wash codes and other information on the tickets, because washing or dry cleaning could also be a deciding factor in your choice.

Colour is the second important consideration. When you are buying for fashion you will take seasonal colours into account – but always hold the fabric to your face in front of a mirror *in the shop* to make sure it suits your personal colouring. Sometimes you will purchase a one-off colour for a dress or special outfit. However, if the garment has to be part of your mix-and-match wardrobe ensure that the colours all tone, match or contrast successfully. If necessary, take one or two items from your wardrobe on your shopping expedition: *never* risk holding colours in your mind, because there are so many shades of most colours.

In household sewing the colour choice is equally important. If you cannot take a sample of furnishing colour with you (perhaps you are matching or toning with a carpet!) then take a fabric snip that does match the item, or a reel of thread of the right colour.

Colouring is important for visual effect. Dark colours can be slimming, whilst loud hot colours like scarlet can emphasize size. Blues and greens are cool colours, but pinks and reds are warm. Yellows and oranges are bright and cheerful, but dark sludgy colours can be dreary and depressing. Learn how to offset the neutral colours with colourful accessories, and how to enliven or brighten a dark room with contrasting touches of colour. If you want to play with colour co-ordinating before you purchase, try experimenting with the colour charts supplied by paint manufacturers.

Textures, patterns and plains provide important detail. Mixing plains with patterns or stripes, or fabrics of varying textures, is fun and can create interest. In fashion, remember that big prints can overwhelm little ladies: stripes can make you look taller, and circular (horizontal) stripes can make you look fatter. Larger women can look very striking in outfits with large prints or patterns. If you have a particularly large area to disguise, use a plain or darker fabric. For example, if you have a small bust and larger hips the proportions will look better with a plain darker skirt and a brightly patterned blouse or bodice (Figure 2.1).

The same types of rules apply in dressing a room. Darker fabrics can recede into the distance, but strong bright colours will bring the feature (such as a window or a chair) into foreground prominence. Large prints will overpower small windows. Vertical stripes will add height and horizontal stripes will add width to the room. Do not mix too many patterns in one room: differently patterned carpet, upholstery and curtains can prove hideous in combination. If you want patterns in all of these areas, seek out mix-and-match designs to give an overall effect which will be easy on the eye.

I think that colour co-ordination is the single most important factor for getting the best out of an outfit or room setting.

The weight and finish of the fabric must be considered. Soft, fluid fabrics will drape well in dress or housecraft, whereas heavier, stiffer fabrics will give added bulk and crispness to the finished article. It is essential to unwind the bolt or roll of fabric in the shop to see how it falls. For a dress, unroll the length of your garment and hold it against you in front of the mirror, unroll a similar length for curtains. Take into account whether or not there will be any lining used, and whether this should be soft or crisp. Remember that interfacing will also affect the structure of various points, such as collars and tabs. Interfacing can be used to strengthen or stiffen lightweight fabrics in housecraft. For example, a good soft draping fabric for curtains can be stiffened with interfacing for the tie-backs.

Durability can be affected enormously by fibre content. Some natural fabrics are stronger than others. Man-made fabrics have different properties. The addition of synthetics can prolong the lives of fabrics, reduce creasing, and make them moth resistant or flame-proof. Weave too is important. For example, a twill weave will be stronger than some flat weaves, and a double knit will usually be more stable than a jumper knit. If you are unsure about the suitability of your choice, seek the advice of the assistant.

To protect your fabric and prolong the life of your outfit or household item, always check on the washing or cleaning requirements and adhere to them rigorously. It is not worth taking a chance on this – *ever*. Remember, too, to avoid using both washable fabrics and those that need dry cleaning in one garment or project: always use fabrics of like fibres together for good results.

2.1 Fabric and figure

TYPES OF FABRIC

Fibres are the basic ingredient from which fabric is made. Fibres are either short, thread-like pieces of animal or vegetable substance spun together to form a yarn which is woven or knitted; or continuous filaments – such as silk and man-made fibres – which do not require spinning. Sometimes the continuous man-made filaments will be chopped into small lengths and spun to reproduce the textures of natural fibres. Amazing advances have been made in recent years in fabric technology, and many man-made fabrics are hard to distinguish from their natural cousins just by looking at and handling them. When the fibres are spun together they make a *yarn*, which is a continuous strand or thread which can be either woven or knitted. Three words are used to denote the end product when these yarns are combined. Technically, *cloth* is a term for woollen woven fabrics; *fabric* is any woven, knitted or felted (non-woven) end product; and *material* applies to cloth or fabric. In common usage all these terms have become interchangeable.

WOOL

PURE NEW WOOL

Wool grows from follicles in the sheep's skin, just as hair grows from human skin. Like human hair, wool is made from the protein keratin, which itself is composed of the most common chemical elements (carbon, oxygen, nitrogen, hydrogen and sulphur) – but the similarity ends there. Because of the wool fibre's unusual construction, the qualities that make wool so useful are genetically built into every hair on the sheep.

In cross-section, each wool fibre consists of a two-part outer layer and an absorbent core. The outer regulates the fibre's dual ability to repel liquid yet absorb moisture. Under a microscope, the outer layer consists of a thin porous sheath which covers overlapping scales that act like tiny roof tiles. These scales cause liquid to bead and roll off the surface of the wool fabric. While this membrane can repel liquid (like moderate rain or a spill), wool absorbs moisture (such as water vapour air humidity or perspiration) through the porous coating over the scales. Through this unique arrangement, wool can absorb up to 30 per cent of its own weight in moisture – without feeling clammy or damp. Thus wool remains absorbent and comfortable inside because its outer surface releases this moisture through evaporation.

Although shorn wool is no longer 'alive' and growing, it does retain the unique life-like action of its thirsty centre cells always striving to stay in balance with the surrounding moisture conditions. This is why wool is said to breathe.

Wool owes many of its other properties to another special trait – its natural crimp. Wool fibres grow permanently crimped, like powerful springs. This permits each fibre to return instantly to its natural posi-

2.2 Wool fabrics (McCabe)

tion after stretching. As a result, wool has enormous elasticity and resilience and can be bent and twisted again and again without breaking.

When wool is woven or knitted, its crimp also creates millions of microscopic air pockets throughout the fabric, giving it lift and creating an insulating layer of air. (As much as 60–80 per cent of wool fabric volume may be entrapped air.)

Wool's unusual ability to regulate moisture and its coiled spring resiliency form the base for many of wool's natural properties and comfort characteristics.

◆ THE PROCESSING OF BRITISH WOOL

Shearing

Shearing takes place once a year, usually during the early summer. Once the sheep have been shorn the wool is collected from the farm by the British Wool Marketing Board and taken to one of its regional centres to be graded into fleece types and qualities.

Grading

The individual fleeces are graded according to the breed type, fibre quality and degree of lustre. Contamination impurities such as vegetable matter, paint and tar are identified at this stage and the fleece graded accordingly.

Scouring

After sorting the wool is then passed through the scouring and washing plant where five different washes remove the natural grease and other foreign matter. A by-product of scoured wool is lanolin, which is extracted from the grease and is used in the manufacture of fine soaps and cosmetics.

Carding

The object of carding is to separate and straighten the long fibres whilst eliminating vegetable matter such as twigs and burs. The carding marchine produces a continuous ribbon of loose fibres approximately the thickness of one's wrist, known as carded sliver.

After carding the wool will proceed in two ways depending on whether it is to become a woollen cloth or a worsted one.

Spinning: woollen process

Spinning for the woollen process produces a softer, bulkier handle to the yarn; worsted spinning produces a stronger, finer quality yarn. A considerable quantity of yarn produced by the woollen process goes into knitting wools and knitted products.

Knitting

Knitting is the process of looping a continuous yarn in vertical lines by means of needles to form a fabric. There are two basic stitches which make a knitted fabric – plain and purl – and there are many fancy stitches and patterns which can be made from them. Knitting can be done by hand on knitting needles or by hand-operated or automatic machines. Knitted fabrics can be cut and sewn for dressmaking on domestic machines and overlockers.

Spinning: worsted process

After a further combing process the carded top is drawn into a finer ribbon and a slight twist is added; this is then called a roving. The roving is placed on to the spinning frame and drawn out and twisted into a fine single-ply yarn. Depending on the end use, the yarn can be twisted on the twisting frame to form two-, three- or multiple-ply yarn.

Weaving

Cloth is woven by first placing the warp yarn (the length of the cloth) on to the loom. The shuttle then carries the weft yarn (the width of the cloth) at high speed through various combinations of the warp, producing different patterns and textiles according to the design required.

Yarn spun by the woollen or worsted process is usually for a specific end product. However, depending on the finish required, worsted yarn can be used for certain knitted garments and vice versa.

◆ ADVANTAGES OF WOOL

The International Wool Secretariat (IWS) advises that wool has many advantages in addition to the evaporation and moisture absorption described earlier. In particular, wool resists:

◇ *Abrasion* Many wools feel soft and can be woven into delicate-looking fabrics, yet possess good durability. Wool can retain its original appearance longer than many other fabrics. It can withstand abrasion and contact with hard surfaces (like the seat of a chair) and still look better than other fabrics, and its resiliency provides a cushion against hard wear.

◇ *Tearing* Wool fibre is so flexible it can be stretched up to 40 per cent beyond its original length before it breaks. This makes wool fabric extremely difficult to tear. When the stress is removed, the natural crimp causes the fibres to spring back into place.

◇ *Crocking* Crocking is the rubbing off and fading of dyes. Wool fibres absorb and hold dyes with lasting ability.

◇ *Snagging* When fabrics catch and snag on something sharp, many tend to pucker; in most cases the snag is permanent. With wool a snag is never long, and snagged fibres can often be flattened out by sponging and pressing the fabric. The fibrous nature of wool fabric surfaces also tends to camouflage short snags.

◇ *Pilling* Pilling is caused when fibres break or work loose on the surface of a fabric and collect into tight and unsightly balls or pills. This can be a major problem with some man-made fabrics.

◇ *Wrinkling* Because of its permanent in-built tendency to spring back into its original shape, wool is difficult to wrinkle. Even when a wool fabric has been packed down for days in a crowded suitcase, most wrinkles disappear on their own after the garment is hung for a while where it can breath.

◇ *Static* Because wool naturally absorbs moisture from the air, it does not offer the dry friction conditions which encourage the build-up of static electricity in clothes. The tendency for clothes to cling and spark is reduced with wool.

◇ *Dirt* Wool stays clean longer than other fabrics because there is less static in wool and thus it does not attract lint and dust from the air. Additionally, wool's crimped fibres and their surface scale structure help keep dirt from penetrating the fibre. Dirt caught in the springy surface hairs can usually be brushed off easily.

Moreover, wool is:

◇ *Flame resistant* Wool is naturally safe because there is moisture in every fibre. Thus it resists flame without chemical treatment.

◇ *Versatile* Wool cloth's excellence of drape is a major asset and has given it a reputation for ease of tailoring. Drape is the way that the cloth fits the body and its movements – the supple and flexible character of a fabric. Wool cloth is easy to work with and can be steamed into shape for a variety of styling effects.

◆ WOOL FABRICS AND FINISHES

As already mentioned, wool fabrics may be divided into two categories according to whether the fibres in the yarn are in a parallel (worsted) or a criss-cross (woollen) relationship. Examples of worsted fabrics are serge, gabardine and crêpe; examples of woollen fabrics are tweed, melton and velour (see the fabric A–Z at the end of this part).

To construct the cloth the warp and weft threads forming the fabric are interlaced with one another according to the structure and design required (Figure 2.4). Three popular forms of interlacing are plain weave, twill and sateen. Plain weave is the most common of all weaves and it gives the strongest fabrics. Twill weaves are also very widely used; they give a heavier fabric than plain weave and a diagonal appearance to the fabric. Sateen

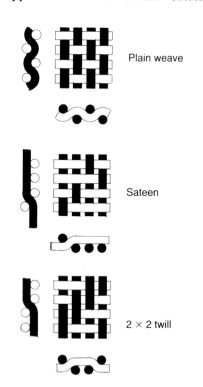

2.3 Interlacing of threads to give three popular weaves

Plain weave

Sateen

2 × 2 twill

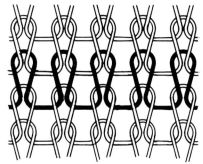

2.4 Weft knitting

weaves are not as popular as the other two, giving a somewhat weaker fabric. Sateen weave is often used as a base on which to build more complicated structures such as crêpe, but it is also used in its own right to produce smooth fabrics of high lustre.

Wool is also made into knitted fabrics (as opposed to jumper knits). There are two methods of knitting: weft knitting (Figure 2.5), where loops are formed by a single yarn passing horizontally across the fabric; and warp knitting (Figure 2.6), where a parallel series of threads is wrapped simultaneously round the knitting needles forming loops which are in a vertical direction. Wool knits can be plain, rib, jacquard, patterned, lacy, single or double jersey, and plush.

Shrink-resistant finishes for wool have been extensively developed over the past two decades. Without such a finish, wool fibres will felt when agitated in water, causing the fabric to shrink in size. Untreated wools should be dry cleaned, and knits given very gentle washing, as described later. Modern methods of polymer-based shrink-resistant processes are comparatively new, but are so successful that many wool fabrics can now be machine washed.

Products carrying the machine-washable wool label (a trade mark of the IWS) are fully machine washable, and will not shrink when machine washed according to the manufacturer's instructions. Equally important, the dyestuffs on the products have been carefully selected so that they will not bleed and stain other garments during washing.

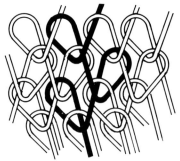

2.5 Warp knitting

◇ *Woolmark* This is the IWS symbol for products made from pure new wool produced to its quality specifications. Woolmark products must be entirely made from new (virgin) wool, except that 5 per cent of other fibres may be added for decorative effect.
◇ *Woolblendmark* This IWS symbol denotes quality-tested goods that are rich in wool. See Figure 2.7.
◇ *Cool wool* is a luxury fabric woven from very fine Woolmark yarns, spun from highest-quality merino wool. A little extra care is needed with these fabrics, and sometimes they take a little longer to shed creases. However, general wool care rules can be followed.

◆ CARING FOR WOOL

The golden rule for wool care must be to check any swing-ticket/label instructions from the manufacturer regarding washing or dry cleaning. If in doubt, test wash, dry and press an off-cut of fabric.

Before you wash any wool garment, turn it inside out. This pro-

2.6 Woolmark and woolblendmark

tects the surface and prevents loose fibres (or the tissue somebody left in a pocket) from ending up on show.

Hand washing

Wash in lukewarm water (40°C). Make sure your powder or liquid is fully dissolved or mixed before immersing the garment. Do exactly as the detergent instructions tell you. Gently squeeze the liquid through the garment a few times. Remember, wool cleans easily. Rinse thoroughly in warm water to remove detergent, and then in cold water. Short spin.

A short (2 minute) soak will also help remove dirt.

Machine washing

First check the fabric label or swing ticket to see that it is all right to machine wash. Follow the washing machine instruction book. If you can not find specific instructions for your machine, use the wash programme coded 7 – a mild wash lasting 2–3 minutes at 40°C.

With a top-loading machine make sure the detergent is completely dissolved before adding the clothes. Rinse and spin dry as usual. Use fabric conditioners if you wish, following the maker's instructions.

Drying

After spin drying, coax the garment back to size and shape while it is still damp.

Drying flat is best. But if you are using a clothes line, fold the garment over it to avoid stretching. Do not peg it up like a shirt. With heavy things it can be a good idea to peg up the sleeves.

Be particularly careful with white and light-coloured garments. *Never* dry them in sunlight or very strong summer daylight or they may discolour. Do not dry any wool item in front of an open or gas or electric fire. And never tumble-dry wool unless the label says you can.

Ironing

Most wool garments benefit from gentle ironing. Use the two dot setting for dry ironing (using a damp cloth will avoid glazing) or lightly iron on the steam setting.

Bleaching

All bleaches discolour and damage wool and should never be used.

Dry cleaning

Most wool garments can be dry cleaned, but check the label. If particular marks and stains look likely to be difficult, point them out to the dry cleaner and ask his or her opinion.

LINEN

 Linen has been serving the needs of mankind for more than 10 000 years. By the time of the Pharaohs its cultivation was already a high art, and the weaving was so fine that they and their queens wore it in stately ceremonies. Fine linen continued to be favoured as part of the rich garb of the Middle Ages and the Renaissance period, and today is still classed as one of the luxury fabrics.

Linen is made from stem fibres of the flax plant. The cultivated species is *Linum usitatissimum* – an apt description, for every part of the plant has its use in industry or fashion.

The name 'flax' is derived from *flacks*, the German name for the plant which in France was known as *lin* and in Italy as *lino*. It has the distinction of being the only natural fibre indigenous to Western Europe.

2.7 Linen fabrics (McCabe)

Today it is mainly grown in France, Belgium and the Netherlands.

The growing of flax requires a temperate, moist climate and good soil. It only requires 100 days from sowing to harvesting, which is done by pulling (not cutting) when the slim plant has grown to a metre and turned a rich straw-brown.

Pressing the fibre into a fabric is a long, costly and labour-intensive process. There are five stages after harvesting:

◇ *Retting* The partial decomposure by moisture of the crop to degrade the natural gums that hold the fibre to the straw.

◇ *Scutching* Beating the woody part of the straw from the fibre.

◇ *Hackling* A combing process to separate short fibre, which goes into tow and is used for coarser fabrics and upholstery, and the longer fibre or line used for sheetings, handkerchiefs and fine dress fabrics.

◇ *Spinning* Either a dry or a wet process depending on the fineness of the yarn required.

◇ *Weaving* Into the wide variety of linen fabrics available.

Linen has very desirable properties which make it comfortable to wear as well as very fashionable:

1 It looks good and keeps its good looks.
2 Of all the textile fibres it washes best. When linen is washed a minute micro-molecular layer is removed from around each fibre. With each wash the surface comes up new without affecting the strength or durability. It is the strongest natural fibre.
3 It is sensitive to moisture and can absorb up to one-fifth of its dry weight of water without feeling damp on the surface. It also gives up its moisture into the surrounding atmosphere more rapidly than any other textile. That is why it is so comfortable to wear in warm or humid weather.
4 Unlike most other textiles, linen yarns and fabrics increase in strength when wet. This is one reason why they wash so well.

Linen can be successfully used in fashion, crafts and home furnishings.

◆ CARING FOR LINEN

Washing

Wash by hand or machine in hot water. Dry and iron whilst slightly damp with a hot iron. Follow wash code tag of garment if appropriate.

Dry cleaning

Dry cleaning is recommended for skirts, jackets and coats in heavier weights of linen.

Removing statins

Giving stains prompt attention is a most important step in removing them. Do not plunge a badly stained article straight into a washing machine without first trying to remove the stain.

◇ *Grease, oil, gravy, butter* Use warm thick suds on stains, rub between hands, wash and rinse.

◇ *Tea and coffee* Remove stain at once. Stretch linen taut over a bowl, pour boiling water on stain from a height.

◇ *Egg* Soak in cold water. Wash and rinse.

◇ *Cream and milk* Wash immediately in cold water. Wash and rinse.

◇ *Tomato juice and ketchup* Sponge thoroughly with cold water. Wash in hot suds and rinse.

◇ *Ink and rust* On white linen, remove with salts of lemon. Remember, salts of lemon are poisonous.

◇ *Fruit and wine* Cover stain at once with salt. As soon as possible, stretch taut linen over a bowl and pour on boiling water. If unsuccessful, rub stain with lemon juice and salt and pour on boiling water.

◇ *Candle wax* Rub with an ice cube. Gently scrape off excess wax. Place cloth between several layers of face tissue or blotting paper and press with hot iron. Remove as much grease as possible this way and then pour boiling water through fabric from a height.

◇ *Alcohol* Soak as soon as possible with cold water, then with a mixture of cold water and glycerine. If stain persists, rinse for a few seconds with vinegar.

◇ *Indelible lipstick* Rub lard into stain. Sponge with dry-cleaning fluid. Wash in warm suds and rinse.

◇ *Blood stains* Soak immediately in cold water. For stubborn blood stains soak the linen for half an hour in a solution of two teaspoonsful of peroxide to a gallon of soapy water, then wash the linen in the normal way.

◇ *Grass stains* Place a pad of cotton wool under the stain and rub it gently with methylated spirit; then wash the garment.

SILK

Silk

The history of silk disappears into the past. It is told that the Chinese Empress Hsi Ling, in 2640 BC, discovered that the cocoons on her mulberry trees were formed from a fine fibre which could be woven into cloth. The secret of producing silk was closely guarded by the Chinese, and it was only as the merchant caravans began to travel across the mountains that silk became known to the West.

At first silk was treated as a trading commodity on a par with gold and precious gems. The finest clothes and furnishings of the most noble European and Mediterranean families came to be made in wonderful silks. There are examples of the fine workmanship of these early times in museums and palaces across the world, and documents of *c*.1600 mention items of 'silke' in the wardrobe of Queen Elizabeth I.

Modern silk usually comes from China and other Far Eastern countries, who supply raw silk for weaving and printing by the most famous fabric houses. Silk is a favourite with couture designers for clothes and accessories. Heavier silk is also used to lavish effect by furnishing experts and interior designers.

Sericulture (the production of silk) is still the same as it was those thousands of years ago, although it is now commercially and scientifically controlled and mechanized. First the *Bombyx mori* moth, which feeds only on mulberry leaves, in late spring lays 400–500 tiny eggs. These hatch into minute silkworms about 2 mm long. During the next month the silkworms grow to around 70–80 mm on a continuous diet of mulberry leaves, shedding their skin four times as they grow out of it.

Having reached their maximum size, they produce their cocoons by

2.8 Silk fabrics (McCabe)

extruding threads from two glands in their head. The threads, fibroin, merge with a gummy substance called sericin, which form the cocoons by binding the threads together. Because the worm moves its head from side to side the cocoon is built up in a series of figure-eight shapes hardened by the sericin. When complete the cocoon is about 3 cm long, white and in the shape of a peanut.

Inside the cocoon the silkworm changes into a chrysalis and then a moth. It produces a brown solution to soften the sericin to enable it to break free. In due course the moth mates, the female lays eggs and the cycle recommences. The life span of the moth is short, ceasing when the eggs are laid.

To escape the cocoon the moth must break the tightly woven threads. To obtain the precious thread unbroken, the producers kill the moth (by various methods including hot air and steam) before it can emerge. After this the cocoon is put into hot water to soften the sericin and ungum the threads. The end of the thread is found, and it is reeled off as a continuous filament into skeins or hanks: over 1000 metres can be reeled off one cocoon.

The wide variety of silk fabrics depends upon the way the threads are then processed. Several threads can be used together or twisted in different ways before the fibre reaches the weaving stage. Although the production of silk is now mechanized, the fineness of the thread, all various processes involved, and the meticulous inspection and finishing mean that it is still a slow labour-intensive process, which accounts for the high cost of fine silk fabrics.

Because silk is so precious, even little pieces of waste fibre and cocoon are gathered up. These tiny pieces of fibre are softened, combed and twisted into a thread and woven. The fabric thus obtained is knobbly, often with dark pieces (fragments of the cocoon) woven into it. This type of silk is called noil silk. Other spun silks have a smooth texture.

◆ SEWING SILK

1 Have confidence when sewing silk! A nervous hand when cutting out or sewing silk can do a lot of damage. If you confidently sew *other* fabrics you will find silk no more of a problem.
2 Use fine pins.
3 Use a pure silk thread where possible. Alternatively use Sylko Supreme, which has an elasticity to match that of the fabric.
4 Use a fine needle, such as 70 (11).
5 When sewing very fine silk, such as chiffon, tack the pieces on to tissue paper and sew through the two layers. For small areas, Stitch-and-Tear can be used.
6 If you have to line the garment use a fine silk such as Jap silk.

7 Test tension, feet, needles etc. on an offcut of fabric before stitching the garment.
8 Any hand stitching should be done with a very fine needle.
9 Press with a warm iron at each stage of construction: give a careful press to the completed garment.

Heavier silks for suits or furnishing items can confidently be sewn using the same rules: however, a heavier needle and interfacing will be necessary. See Part 4 for needles, threads and interfacings.

MOHAIR

Mohair is the fleece of the Angora goat, a gentle animal known since the beginning of human history. Nowadays it is principally reared in Argentina, Australia, Lesotho, New Zealand, South Africa, Texas and Turkey.

However, as to the origins of the Angora goat there appears to be a certain amount of mystery and speculation. The Angora goat derives its name from the province of Angora in Turkey, and it was in 1550 that a Dutchman travelling in that area saw the goats and immediately recognized the exceptional quality of the fleece. Similar white-haired goats were also sighted in the Himalayas and it is quite possible that they had been driven or wandered from Tibet into Asia Minor. The Turks, too, realized the potential of mohair, and jealously guarded their flocks of Angoras.

Outside interest in the fibre grew. Demand exceeded supply, which led the Sultan to forbid the export of raw mohair. In an effort to meet this growing demand, the Turks decided to cross the Angora goat with the native Kurdish goat. The quality naturally declined and the pure Angora ran the risk of extinction.

In 1838, under pressure from England, the export ban was lifted, and mohair became known to a much wider extent in Europe but only in the form of spun yarns. Many attempts were made to export the actual goats, but these failed owing to the delicate nature of the beast. It was found that Angora goats could only live in a warm, dry climate. This climate was found in

2.9 Mohair fabrics (McCabe)

South Africa, and in 1839 the first Angora goats were successfully shipped to that country, which is now one of the world's leading mohair producers.

It was almost by chance that Angora goats came to the USA, where they were mistakenly imported as Kashmir goats. The Southern Agricultural Society investigated the matter and confirmed that the goats were in fact Angoras. In this way, the Angora spread to many parts of the States, but few areas were suitable for breeding. Today only Texas, where the Angora goat can thrive, is important in the production of mohair.

Because the Angora goat can live only in specialized climatic conditions, and as a result of its superb qualities, mohair will always remain an exclusive, luxurious material, second to none.

There are 6–7 million Angora goats in the world. Each animal provides on average 2 kg of hair when shorn. The total output of mohair, however, is a mere 0.25 per cent of all natural fibres. The handling of these fibres remains the province of a few. The mohair is skilfully sorted, washed, combed, spun and woven by craftsmen. To regain its natural resilience, the fibre is rested at intervals; the longer it takes to process mohair, the better the final product.

The fibre's natural, white, silky smooth, lustrous characteristics allow it to dye easily, vibrantly and lastingly in any shade. Mohair also takes kindly to anything up to a dozen special finishing techniques that highlight its smooth-as-water softness in some fabrics and cool, dry texture in others. Some mohair is made into textiles in the Angora's home countries, but it is mostly shipped overseas where it is made into yarns, fabrics, garments and furnishings.

Mohair is made into many things: men's suitings, gossamer scarves, exclusive furnishing velour, fluffed-up fabric for ladies' wear, and subtle hand-knitting yarns.

◆ CARING FOR MOHAIR

1 Hang up your mohair garments after wear so that they can relax and regain perfect shape.
2 Brush regularly: this helps to prolong the life of the garment.
3 Always empty pockets when not in use.
4 Never skimp on dry cleaning: use an expert.

COTTON

Cotton is grown mainly as an annual plant to a height of between 25 cm and 2 m. The seed pods, or bolls, develop from the fertilised flowers of the plant hairs. The bolls continue to grow for about two months until they ripen and burst open to reveal the fluffy mass of fibres which, after separation from the seed, is known as cotton lint. Each boll contains about 30 seeds, and each seed produces from 2000 to 7000 fibres.

Between 175 and 225 frost-free days are needed traditionally for successful cultivation, because cotton is sensitive to cold weather conditions. However, new intensive methods of cultivation in the USA and elsewhere can shorten the growing season to as few as 135 days. At the same time agronomists are developing varieties of cotton to suit intensive cultivation techniques whereby the cotton bolls can all reach a state of maturity together, to permit once-and-for-all harvesting.

Harvesting is spread over some 30 days to allow the cotton fibres to mature and dry out. The cotton is then subjected to the ginning process, which separates the fibres from the seed. From 100 kg of seed cotton the yield is about 35 kg of fibres, 62 kg of seed and 3 kg of waste material. The raw cotton is then compressed into bales, usually of 230 kg, which are wrapped and secured by metal bands.

Raw cotton varies considerably in quality and in the average length of the individual fibres. It is bought principally on the basis of fibre length (staple). Important quality considerations include uniformity, fineness, colour, purity, handle, strength and elasticity. Principal faults are excessive impurities and a high content of short, immature, deformed or dead fibres.

Its character depends on the type of cotton and the environment in which it is gown. The finest long-staple cotton, known as Sea Island, comes from the West Indies. Long and extra long staple cottons are grown mainly in Egypt and the Sudan, and some also in Peru. The USA provides strong medium-staple varieties, while Indian cotton is mainly of short staple. In nearly all the cotton-producing countries, research and development is being carried out to improve both the quality and the yield of cotton crops.

Cotton fibres vary in length from about 15 to 42 mm. The maximum thickness of the individual cotton fibre varies between 12 and 45 μm (thousandths of a millimetre, or microns).

Cotton fabric types include denim, canvas, corduroy, velvet, poplin, seersucker, lace, chambray, shirtings, sweatshirting, moleskin, lawn, chintz, organdie, gaberdine and jersey.

2.10 Cotton fabrics (McCabe)

◆ THE PROCESSING OF COTTON

When raw cotton arrives at a mill it is cleaned, carded and combed. This ensures that all the fibres are lying in the same direction. Automatic spinning by ring or rotor machines collects the yarns on to bobbins or discs in preparation for weaving or knitting.

Cloth straight from the loom is known as loom-state or grey, and because it still contains some impurities and discoloration it is washed and bleached. These processes make the cotton fibres clean and absorbent – these are perfect conditions for dying and printing. Finishing, by definition, is the final process which can be anything from ironing the fabric to make it crease resistant or water repellant. It can be brushed, crinkled, stone washed, overdyed, clipped or sueded. Cotton can be woven into denim, corduroy, velvet, lace, canvas, poplin, gaber-dine, voile or lawn, and knitted into most weights from lacy lingeries to fleecy sweatshirt jersey.

The finished fabrics are made into all types of clothing with the fabrics developing to keep ahead of fashion trends. Cotton is also used for protective suits, uniforms, household furnishings, shoes, umbrellas, tents, handkerchiefs, towels, bandages and so on.

Even cotton rags are reprocessed and used in the manufacture of banknotes; cotton seed is crushed and used as animal feed; and cotton linters (the tiny hairs left on the seed) are made into string, wicks, carpet yarn, mattress stuffing, domestic upholstery, explosives, films, plastics and paper. Cotton seed is also refined to produce cooking oil and flour for human consumption.

Around the world, some 14 million tonnes of cotton are produced and used each year. Cotton is uni-que and has properties which are impossible to duplicate. With proper care it lasts years; the oldest example of cotton fabric dates from 5800 BC.

◆ ADVANTAGES OF COTTON

The International Institute for Cotton advises that cotton is:

◇ *Healthy* The natural fibre readily absorbs moisture. It will take up to 40 per cent of its own weight of water. Moreover, under normal conditions cotton fabric rapidly dispels moisture by evaporation. This continual process of moisture absorption and evaporation makes cotton pleasant and comfortable to wear and is an important health factor because it allows the skin to breathe freely.

◇ *Clean* All textile fibres to a greater or lesser extent acquire small charges of static electricity due to friction when they are in use. They therefore attract tiny dust particles which soil the fabrics, and in some fibres this can be difficult to remove. Cotton is one of the fibres on which static electricity accumulates much less rapidly, and is therefore one of the easiest to keep clean.

◇ *Fresh* One of its greatest charms is freshness. It is so easy to wash and iron. Cotton can be boiled without harming the fibres and the water can penetrate right to the core of the fibre so all the dirt is washed out. However, always adhere to the washing instructions. Cotton is also mothproof!

◇ *Strong* The individual cotton hairs are surprisingly strong. Even the finest and lightest of fabrics, such as voile and lawn, wear exceptionally well and can be repeatedly washed without damage. Cotton is even stronger wet than dry.

◇ *Versatile* Cotton has a great affinity for chemicals and can therefore take a multitude of different finishes. It can be woven or knitted into almost any texture and dyed to any colour. It can be made shrink and crease resistant, and water and stain repellent. It can be glazed, embossed, waterproofed, printed, brushed or mercerized.

◆ CARING FOR COTTON

Laundering

One of cotton's greatest virtues is that it is easy and safe to wash. It is better to wash frequently before articles become really dirty. Follow the washing instructions where given on labels. Use only the specified amount of washing powder or detergent. Most household whites can be boiled and may be bleached to remove stains. Wash yellow dusters separately.

Fabrics likely to bleed colour (reds and blacks are the most likely) should be washed separately or dry cleaned. Colour fastness can be tested by placing the wet fabric or garment between two pieces of white cotton and pressing dry with a hot iron.

After washing, rinse throughly. Articles should be rinsed and squeezed until the water is clear and free from soap or detergent. A dash of vinegar added to rinsing water will brighten printed cottons. A small quantity of borax may be added to the rinse in hard water areas. Starching restores crispness to those cotton fabrics that require it. A plastic starch will last through several washings: follow the instructions on the packet.

Most cottons should be ironed on the face side to bring up their natural sheen. Embossed or embroidered cottons should be pressed face side down, preferably on a padded cloth.

Particular attention to instructions given on labels should be paid when laundering easy-care cottons to determine the recommended wash temperature, the type and amount of washing powder, and whether (in the case of whites) bleach may be used. In some easy-care finishes, non-bleachable resins are used, and these may cause the fabric to yellow or retain a strong chlorine odour after washing. Line dry or tumble easy-care cottons.

Wash cotton velvets and corduroys in lukewarm water with mild soap flakes. Do not rub or wring out. Allow to drip dry, preferably in the open air. While the garment is drying it should be pulled gently into shape. When nearly dry the pile should be brushed lightly with a soft brush. Then stand an iron upright and draw the back of the cloth across the face of the iron. Flattened pile can be raised and freshened without washing by hanging the garment in a steamy atmosphere, or by judicious use of the steam from a kettle (remember to don protective gloves).

Knitted cotton outerwear should be washed in lukewarm water with the mildest of soap flakes. Wash quickly without undue rubbing or wringing. Rinse, squeeze gently and dry flat after spreading the garment out to correct shape.

Remove surface dirt and dust from curtain fabrics and loose covers before washing. Check for wash fastness with colours. Avoid excessive rubbing and rinse well.

Stain removal

Stains should be treated as soon as possible. Cotton's natural absorbency allows bleach and other household solvents to penetrate quickly and remove stains effectively. Check with colours that they are fast to bleaching. If bleach is used to remove a stain, use only the amount recommended by the manufacturer. The most widely used bleach is chlorine, available under a variety of brand names in either liquid or powder form.

Oxygen-type bleaches, such as hydrogen peroxide and sodium perborate, are usually as effective as the chlorine types and are especially recommended in removing stains from easy-care fabrics to avoid discoloration. With sodium perborate use a solution of one tablespoon of bleach to one cup of warm water. In treating more stubborn stains, the garment may be boiled for approximately 20 minutes in a solution of one tablespoon of sodium perborate

to two cups of water, and then washed in the usual fashion. Hydrogen peroxide should be used in a concentration of at least 15 per cent. Sodium perborate, however, is less harmful to the skin than either the chlorine-type bleach or hydrogen peroxide, and is most effective.

Certain easy-care fabrics which have not been treated with a non-chloride retentive finish will turn yellow if washed with a chlorine-type bleach. This yellowing can usually be removed by soaking the fabric in a solution of two tablespoons of sodium sulphite and half a cup of white vinegar in a gallon of water. Soak for a few minutes and rinse throughly. Sodium sulphite can be bought in chemists or photographic supply stores. Commercial colour removers can also be used.

Oil-borne stains should first be treated with a household cleaning solvent. Care should be taken not to rub too hard, since this will tend to fix the stain more deeply rather than remove it.

Although most stains can be removed with bleach or a household solvent, many common household stains require special treatment. If there is any question as to the proper method of removing a particular stain, it is recommended that a commercial laundry or dry cleaner be consulted, as improper treatment could set the stain to such an extent that it will be impossible to remove. Certain stains may be set with heat and others even upon contact with water.

Treatment of common household stains on cotton

◇ *Blood* The stain should be soaked overnight in cold water before laundering. The affected area may also be treated in a solution of two tablespoons of ammonia to one gallon of water.
◇ *Fruit and berry stains* Soap should never be used to remove fruit or berry stains. The fruit particles should first be loosened under cool water. The affected area should then

be soaked overnight in clear, cool water before laundering in the usual fashion.

◇ *Grape juice* The affected area should be sprinkled with salt immediately after occurrence and then treated as described below for tea or coffee. Should the stain not be discovered until it has been allowed to dry, moisten the area slightly before sprinkling with salt.

◇ *Ink* Ink stains may be treated with commercial ink remover or dipped in sweet milk and allowed to stand until sour. Caution should be exercised in the use of commercial ink removers, as many brands contain chlorine-type bleaches.

◇ *Lipstick* Lipstick stains can usually be effectively removed with bleach, particularly sodium perborate, and hot, sudsy water. The stain may also be rubbed with lard, which should be scraped off before washing the garment in hot suds.

◇ *Mildew* Mildew stains are the most difficult to remove, but if treated in the very early stages may sometimes be removed with bleach or by the application of salt and lemon juice followed by exposure to sunshine.

◇ *Rust* Rust stains may be dipped in a solution of oxalic acid followed by a thorough rinsing. Salt, lemon juice and sun exposure are also helpful.

◇ *Soft drinks* Sponge the soiled area with water or with detergent and warm water before laundering.

◇ *Tea or coffee* The soiled area should first be stretched over a bowl and then boiling water from a kettle poured through until the stain disappears.

MAN-MADE FABRICS

◆ PRODUCTION OF MAN-MADE FIBRES

All man-made fibres are produced by an extrusion technique. In simplest terms, this could be likened to forcing treacle through the rose of a watering can, then immediately solidifying the thin streams which emerge. Modern techniques are, of course, extremely sophisticated and far more complex. The plate or die with up to thousands of precision drilled holes through which the liquid is forced is called a spinneret. The viscous liquid from which most man-made fibres are produced is usually referred to as the dope or polymer. Theoretically, this viscous liquid could be based on any one, or even more than one, of literally hundreds of different raw materials. Because of the enormous amount of capital investment, time and intensive research involved in perfecting one type of man-made fibre, scientists have tended to choose and concentrate on a mere handful of the most suitable as far as large-scale textile applications are concerned. Nevertheless, more unusual polymers may be used for making small quantities of high-performance

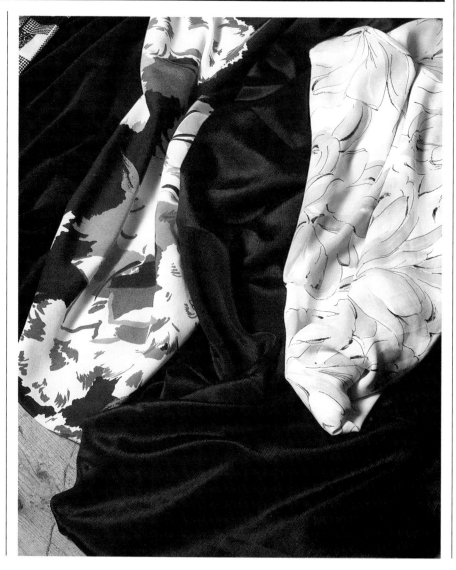

2.11 Man-made fabrics (McCabe)

fibres (usually for more or less specific industrial applications) if the importance of the end use justifies the necessary expense and effort. The ultimate performance and characteristics of the fibres can be decided and modified at this stage; agents are added to the polymer or dope to give colour or special dyeability, antistatic properties, flame retardancy or other characteristics. Sometimes even the shape of the holes in the spinneret is modified to create filaments of special cross-section to improve the characteristics of the fibre for certain applications. (Carpet fibres, for example, are often given a cross-section which actually preserves the appearance of the carpet pile.)

Once the fibres have been extruded through the spinneret and solidified, they are usually drawn (stretched under controlled tension) to orientate the molecules. This drawing produces strength, uniformity and other desirable characteristics. Groups of filaments may then be twisted together to form a continuous filament yarn, or the entire bundle of filaments – called a tow – may be first crimped then chopped into comparatively short lengths (staple fibres) to resemble natural fibres or to suit different spinning systems.

Viscose, the first widely used man-made fibre, is based on regenerated cellulosic materials. Most other man-made fibres are based on products of the petrochemical industry, and are described more precisely as synthetic fibres.

Within the man-made fibres industry, extrusion processes are classified as wet spun, dry spun or melt spun. In wet spinning, the filaments emerge into a chemical bath to be immediately solidified (coagulated). In dry spinning, the filaments are coagulated by emerging from the spinneret into a cabinet filled with heated air which evaporates all solvents. In melt spinning, the polymer is normally fed into the extrusion process as chips or granules and is melted before being forced

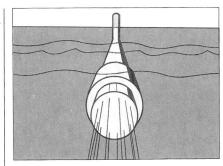

Wet spinning

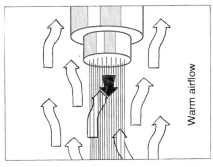

Warm airflow

Dry spinning

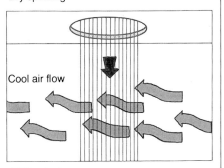

Cool air flow

Melt spinning

2.12 Extrusion processes

through the spinneret to emerge as filaments which are then cooled. Obviously the method is chosen to suit the polymer being processed.

Man-made fibres can usually be modified at any stage during production (with additives such as dyestuffs and dulling agents) or immediately afterwards (by drawing, crimping, or the application of antistat finishes), to suit the end product. The fibres can be created to match the requirements of the textile (not the other way round, as often happens when natural fibres are used). Once engineered to suit a given application, fibre characteristics are identical from batch to batch. Alternatively, if it is not feasible or economic to achieve a desired result by modifying one type

of man-made fibre, different types can be blended together to give required performance.

◆ TYPES OF MAN-MADE FIBRE

In identifying man-made fibres it is important to appreciate the difference between type and brand name. Lycra, for example, is the brand name of an elastane fibre produced by Du Pont.

Many fibre producers make similar types, but each one has its own brand names. Thus polyamide fibres from ICI Fibres may be called Timbrelle or Tactel, while those from Du Pont can be ticketed Antron. Evlan, Viloft and Fibro are different versions of viscose all developed by Courtaulds for different applications. Polyesters produced by ICI may be marketed as Terylene, Terinda or Mitrelle; Hoechst's range of polyesters is marketed as Trevira. Different brand names may be used by one fibre producer for the same generic type of fibre to differentiate between special versions or applications. There are literally thousands of different brand names in use throughout the world. Today most items of clothing identify the type of fibre content; many also carry a fibre brand name.

The following outlines the main properties and uses of different fibre types:

◇ *Acetate and triacetate* yarns are based on a derivative of cellulose. Their performance and properties are however different from those of viscose. Acetate is silk-like, with soft handle and drape. It is used in furnishing fabrics, knitted and woven dresswear and underwear, velvet-like pile fabrics and linings. Triacetate has quick-drying properties and, in addition to being used in similar applications to those for acetate fibres, is well suited for pleated apparel.

◇ *Acrylic* fibres compete with wool in desirable softness. Their comfort and warmth are attractive in knitwear; their pleasing colours are popular in upholstery, velvets and curtains, and carpets. Acrylic fibres are widely used for hand knitting yarns. Garments possess easy-care qualities and maintain appearance over long use. Special versions called modacrylic are inherently flame retardant and are used for furnishings, sleepwear and toys.

◇ *Aramid* fibres and yarns are primarily for industrial products and are among the strongest fibres in the world. Their strength/weight ratio is such that weight for weight they can be five times stronger than steel. They have high thermal and good dimensional stability, and low elongation. They are flame resistant (they will not melt) and do not corrode. Aramid fibres are non-conductive and have excellent dielectric properties. They are used in a widening range of industrial applications from heat-resistant cladding tiles on space vehicles, brake shoes and foundry gloves to tyre belting, cables, lifting bags, conveyor belts and high-pressure hoses. Some versions are used extensively for industrial and ballistic protective clothing.

◇ *Carbon* fibres, now adopted for an increasing variety of high-performance industrial applications, mostly stem from the same polyacrylonitrile base as acrylic fibres. They are being used in applications ranging from fishing rods to aircraft components.

◇ *Elastane* yarns (once known as spandex) offer the highest stretch and recovery performance of any fibre in common use. Based on polyurethane, they resist damage by perspiration and by many chemicals which affect rubber. Their lightness/ performance ratio and their washability have won for elastane a major role in foundation garments and swimwear.

◇ *Polyamide* fibres have developed from the once ubiquitous nylon – of which they were probably more different versions than any other synthetic fibre. Polyamide fibres can be strong yet comfortable, hard wearing yet soft to touch, with ex-

cellent easy-care performance. They are light and versatile, and resist bacteria and many chemicals. Polyamides are one of the most popular fibres for carpets. They are used in demanding industrial applications – tyres, ropes, tenting fabrics – yet are also universally popular for sheer underwear and lingerie, swimwear and hosiery. Sophisticated polyamide yarns have an increasing share of the sportswear market, providing performance, comfort and fashion appeal.

◇ *Polyester* is currently the most widely used man-made fibre, accounting for almost 20 per cent of all fibre used throughout the world. A truly synthetic fibre, it is available in many versions, all of which are strong, non-absorbent and resistant to sunlight. Polyester fabrics are washable and crush resistant. They possess performance and processing qualities demanded in consumer and industrial applications ranging from curtain nets and suitings to conveyor belting and civil engineering constructions. Polyester fibre blends with other man-made fibres (such as viscose) and natural fibres (wool, linen and cotton) to give excellent easy-care and permanent crease properties. It resists moths, damp and chemical degradation.

◇ *Polypropylene* is used in carpets (tufted, woven and needle punched) in upholstery, packaging, sackings, intermediate bulk containers, webbings, geotextiles and various other types of industrial textiles. It can be used alone or in blends with other fibres for some types of apparel. Polypropylene is light, strong and resists soiling and most chemicals.

◇ *Viscose*, the original man-made fibre, is still one of the most important in terms of world usage. Earlier versions were known as rayon – even originally as artificial silk. Today viscose is available in several advanced forms, variously offering outstanding absorbency, strength, comfort, softness and colour. Viscose is used alone or in blends with other man-made or natural fibres in most apparel and many home and

industrial textile applications. It is frequently used in blends with polyester or cotton for fashion apparel and workwear, home textiles, furnishings, and a number of industrial applications.

◆ DEVELOPMENT OF MAN-MADE FIBRE INDUSTRY

The UK man-made fibre industry is one of the most important in Western Europe and is an acknowledged world leader in innovative technology. It produces almost a quarter of all man-made fibres made in Western Europe, supplying both the UK textile industry and overseas customers. Almost half total annual production is exported – with an increasing proportion going to the EEC.

UK scientists were among the first involved in developing man-made fibres and have been associated with virtually every major advance in the technology of their production. As early as 1664 Robert Hooke was investigating the possibility of making a silk-like thread based on a wood-derived cellulose. Two hundred years later Sir Joseph Swan made strands or filaments of fibre by dissolving cellulose and forcing it through fine holes into a chemical bath (his objective was to develop filaments for use in newly invented electric lights – an early appreciation of the potential for man-made fibres in industry). It was in 1889, however, that a French chemist – Count Hilaire de Chardonnet – demonstrated how man-made cellulose filaments could be used to manufacture artificial silk.

In 1904 a UK weaving company, Samuel Courtauld & Co. Ltd, bought British rights for a process to make viscose (at that time known as rayon) fibres from chemically treated wood pulp. A plant for the purpose was built at Coventry, and nine years later a new company – Courtaulds Ltd – was formed to control the viscose fibre operation. Courtaulds has since consistently held a position as one of the world's leading fibre producers and today operates on an international scale.

Acetate, because it is chemically modified regenerated cellulose, could be regarded as an early step on the road to truly synthetic fibres; it was developed in the second decade of this century. Triacetate fibres were evolved from cellulose acetate technology. However, viscose remained by far the most important and successful man-made fibre for 60 years, with more of this type of fibre being made annually during the first half of this century than all other man-made fibres put together.

The first hint of a challenge to the supremacy of viscose came in 1939 with the display of nylon stockings at the San Francisco World Fair. Developed originally by Du Point in the USA, nylon was first produced by a UK company, British Nylon Spinners, as early as 1941. Until the end of the Second World War, output was swallowed by military demands – parachutes, tyres, tents, ropes, and so on. Once supplies became available, post-war nylon rapidly captured the hosiery market, then entered the lingerie business, and – by the mid 1950s – the carpet sector. There are now literally hun-

dreds of different types of these fibres and yarns produced throughout the world. To emphasize the refinement and high performance of the more advanced versions over earlier types of this family of fibres, the term nylon has been supplanted by polyamide.

As the first UK nylon plant moved into commercial production, a second synthetic fibre – polyester – was emerging from the research laboratories of the Calico Printers' Association to be developed commercially by ICI. Polyester fibres are based on two oil derivatives which together make polyethylene terephthalate. As Terylene, this ICI fibre went into large-scale production in 1955. The UK organization also licensed producers in Western Europe and elsewhere to make similar fibres. Hoechst AG, a West German group and one of the licensees for the process, built a Trevira polyester fibre factory in Northern Ireland. Today more polyester fibre is produced internationally than any other synthetic fibre. Polyamide takes second place in terms of volume. The two rarely compete directly: each has found textile areas for which it is best suited.

The third major synthetic fibre – acrylic – was developed in Germany

in the 1940s. Based on polyacrylonitrile, it went into commercial production in the 1950s, and a production facility was set up in the UK by Courtaulds to make Courtelle acrylic fibre in 1957.

Polypropylene fibre was introduced in the mid 1950s, and is particularly suited for small-scale production.

◆ CARING FOR MAN-MADE FABRICS

The most outstanding characteristic of man-made fibre textiles is their easy-care properties.

Most man-made fibre garments are either drip-dry or minimum iron, and can be washed frequently and easily without harming their appearance or performance if a few simple instructions are followed. These care instructions usually appear on the wash care labels, and it is wise to look for such labels when buying.

The problem of clinging garments – caused by static electricity – has been largely cured with today's man-made fibres. If static is encountered, a proprietary fabric conditioner will usually eliminate it.

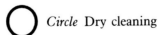

INTERNATIONAL TEXTILE CARE LABELLING CODE

◆ THE CODE

The international textile care labelling code is based on five outline symbols:

 Wash tub The washing process (by machine or hand)

 Triangle Chlorine bleaching

 Circle in square Tumble drying (after washing)

 Iron Ironing

○ *Circle* Dry cleaning

◆ THE WASHING PROCESS

The three variables in the washing process (water temperature, agitation and spinning) are indicated by the tub symbols. Maximum water temperature is shown in degrees Celsius inside the tub. One bar

under the tub means reduced mechanical action and short spin; two bars mean much reduced mechanical action but normal spinning.

The amount of machine agitation is as follows:

◇ *Maximum* wash means the maximum recommended agitation for any machine as defined by its manufacturer.

◇ *Medium* wash means 40–60 per cent of the maximum recommended agitation.

◇ *Minimum* wash means the recommended minimum amount of agitation for any given machine, normally 20–30 per cent of maximum.

In top-loading agitator/pulsator type machines, variation of amount of agitation is normally achieved by control of total wash time. In front-loading automatic machines, variations of one or more of four parameters is used, viz: wash time, wash rhythm during wash, wash rhythm during heating, and water level, which are an integral part of washing machine design.

With the exception of 'short (reduced) spin' the instructions given for water extraction are self-explanatory. 'Short (reduced) spin' is defined as the minimum spinning time recommended by the manufacturer of the particular appliance.

The usual wash tub symbols and their fabric applications are as follows:

 White cotton and linen articles without special finishes

 Cotton, linen or viscose articles without special finishes where colours are fast at 60°C

 (Not used in UK) White nylon and white polyester/cotton mixtures are included in

 Nylon: polyester/cotton mixtures; polyester cotton and viscose articles with special finishes; cotton/acrylic mixtures

 Cotton, linen or viscose articles, where colours are fast at 40°C but not at 60°C

 Acrylics, acetate and triacetate, including mixtures with wool; polyester/wool blends

 Wool, wool mixed with other fibres; silk

 (Not used in UK) See items included in and

 (Not applicable in UK)

 Hand wash (Do not machine wash)

Do not wash

As a general guide you can mix wash labels without a bar, provided you wash at the lowest temperature shown. Likewise, you can mix wash labels with and without a bar provided that you wash at the lowest temperature *and* the least washing action shown. Remember, 'wash separately' means what it says.

Launderettes often have a simpler range of machine settings that make mixing wash loads essential. The same rules apply.

Rinsing instructions are only included when they are of special significance.

◆ CHLORINE BLEACHING

A triangle containing the letters Cl indicates that the article may be treated with chlorine bleach. If it is crossed out this means that chlorine bleach must not be used. The symbol refers to chlorine bleach only and does not apply to other types of bleach. It is most likely to appear on articles and fabrics labelled on the continent where the practice of using chlorine bleach is more common than in the UK.

◆ TUMBLE DRYING AFTER WASHING

The vast majority of textile articles can be safely tumble dried. Important, however, is the need to warn against the use of a tumble dryer if the article is likely to be harmed by this treatment (e.g. articles containing foam rubber or rubber-like materials, most wool knitwear etc.)

◆ IRONING

There are four variations of the ironing symbol, as shown below. The temperatures shown in brackets are the maximum sole plate temperatures indicated by the dots in the symbol.

 Hot (200°C) Cotton, linen, viscose or modal (modified viscose)

 Warm (150°C) Polyester mixtures, wool

 Cool (110°C) Acrylic, nylon, acetate, triacetate, polyester

 Do not iron This symbol should only be used in cases where ironing would be detrimental to the fabric, and *not* on easy-care fabrics to indicate that ironing is not necessary.

In addition to the symbol, in the UK the words 'cool', 'warm' or 'hot' may also appear on the label.

◆ DRY CLEANING

There are also variables which apply to the dry cleaning process, but normally these are not controlled by the owner of the goods to be cleaned. The exception only exists for those using coin-operated dry cleaning machines, who should check that the cleaning symbol shown on the label is the same as that in the instructions given on the front of the machine.

◇ *Circle symbol* The principal part of the dry cleaning symbol is the circle, which means that the garment can be dry cleaned. The circle should never appear on its own. It should always have additional information as follows.

◇ *Symbol variants* Letters are placed in the circle to indicate which types of cleaning solvent may be used. Only the letters A, P and F are recognized: A for all solvents; P for perchloroethylene, white spirit, solvent 113 and solvent 11; and F for white spirit or solvent 113.

(A) Normal goods dry cleanable in all solvents.

(P) Normal goods dry cleanable in perchloroethylene, solvent R113, white spirit and solvent R11.

(P̲) Goods sensitive to dry cleaning which may be cleaned with the same solvent, but with a strict limitation on the addition of water during cleaning are restrictions concerning mechanical action or drying temperature or both.

(F) Normal goods dry cleanable in solvent R113 and white spirit.

(F̲) Goods sensitive to dry cleaning which may be cleaned with the same solvents shown but with a strict limitation on the addition of water during cleaning and/or certain restrictions concerning mechanical action or drying temperature or both.

⊗ dry clean. The cross must be of the shape shown overlying the circle.

◆ EXAMPLES OF THE NEW LABEL FORMATS

[50 wash tub] Wash as Synthetics	MACHINE	HAND WASH
	Hand hot medium wash	Hand hot
	Cold rinse. Short spin or drip-dry	
[bleach crossed]	DO NOT USE CHLORINE BLEACH	
[tumble dry]	MAY BE TUMBLE DRIED	
[iron]	WARM	
(P)	DRY CLEANABLE	

[50 wash tub] [bleach crossed] [tumble dry] [iron] **(P)**
Wash as Synthetics

[50 wash tub] MACHINE OR HAND WASH	**(P)** Dry Cleanable
[bleach crossed] Do not Bleach	[tumble dry] Tumble Dry	[iron] Cool iron

	MACHINE	HAND WASH
[50 wash tub]	Hand hot medium wash	Hand hot
	Cold rinse. Short spin or drip-dry	
	Wash as Synthetics	
[bleach crossed] DO NOT USE CHLORINE BLEACH	[tumble dry] MAY BE TUMBLE DRIED	[iron] WARM IRON	**(P)** DRY CLEAN ABLE

A-Z OF FABRIC TERMS

Acetate A synthetic fibre made from cellulose acetate solution. Acetate can be used alone to give a silky fabric or mixed with other fibres to give extra sheen. If machine embroidery is done on this fabric the acetate background can then be dissolved with acetone to give a lace-like finish.

Acrylic A synthetic fibre made from acrylonitrile, produced from coal, air, water, petroleum and limestone. An extremely lightweight but warm fabric.

Alpaca A luxury fabric. It is considered a wool, although the fibre is a long hair from the llama. It provides a cloth which is soft, silky and light in weight.

Angora The soft, silky hair of the angora rabbit. The hair is sometimes mixed with other woollen fibres to add softness. Angora is used by itself or with other fibres to provide a knitting yarn.

Artificial silk One of the early names for rayon fabric: seldom used now.

Baize A loosely woven fabric which resembles a thin felt. Many traditional uses, but most commonly known for covering card and billiard tables. It can usefully be used for backings, linings and in craft work.

Barathea A traditional wool fabric. It was originally a wool/silk mixture, and today sometimes has a mixture of synthetic fibres. It has a very smooth finish with a broken rib pattern.

Barkcloth Originating in the South Pacific, this fabric was made from the inner bark of certain types of trees. The term is also applied to a modern mixture of cotton and viscose with a crêpe-type finish to resemble genuine barkcloth.

Bark crêpe Another fabric resembling barkcloth, but with a more pronounced or exaggerated effect.

Batiste A very lightweight, soft, sheer fabric which can be made in almost any fibres. Wool batiste is similar to nun's veiling, and cotton and linen batiste are traditional lightweight summer fabrics. Synthetics and blended fibres are also used.

Batting An American term for the wadding used in quilting and other craft techniques.

Benares A lightweight fabric woven with metallic threads: from India.

Bengaline A very strong, closely woven fabric with crosswise ribs. In narrow strips it makes grosgrain ribbon.

Billiard cloth A sturdy but fine twilled fabric of tradition green used to cover billiard tables. Originally made from wool, it may now be made from other fibres.

Bombazine A black twilled fabric traditionally used for mourning clothes in previous eras.

Bonding This term is applied to two fabrics glued or joined together by the application of heat to melt the fibres. Non-woven fabrics and interfacings are made in this way.

Bouclé Refers to a thick, stubbly yarn, although the fabric made from these yarns is also called bouclé. Bouclé fabrics can be knitted or woven and normally have a dull surface; however, shiny yarns may be incorporated as contrast.

Broadcloth A traditional wool term for a light, tightly woven fabric with a soft, slightly napped surface. Mercerized cotton was also extensively used for broadcloth, but today many other fibres can be used.

Brocade A luxurious fabric, heavy in weight and traditionally incorporating a jacquard design of flowers and leaves. Metallic threads are also incorporated for special effects.

Brocatel Also made on a jacquard loom, this fabric is similar to brocade but with a blistered or puffed appearance.

Broderie Anglaise Another name for eyelet embroidery, and the fabric embroidered in this way is usually called by the same name. Traditionally a cotton fabric, but it is now often mixed with synthetic fibres.

Buckram Made from extremely coarse yarns which provide a stiff open weave which is then permanently stiffened. Buckram is used as a shaping interfacing for such items as hats and pelmets.

Buckskin Deer and elk skins provide this inexpensive leather. The term is also applied to a fabric of satin weave with a napped finish.

Bulked fabrics Bulking is a finish often used in knitting yarns but also in such fabrics as Crimplene. Bulking makes the yarn thicker or bulkier, thus giving a less shiny, fluffy appearance.

Calico A traditionally cotton fabric with a smooth surface and plain weave, which now sometimes incorporates other fibres. Useful in crafts and sometimes in fashion.

Cambric Another useful craft fabric, of plain weave but finished with a slightly glossy surface. Traditionally made from cotton or linen, but now mixed with other fibres.

Camel hair A luxury fabric. It is referred to as a wool, although it is the underhair of the camel. To add to the durability of the cloth it is usually mixed with sheep wools and/or other fibres. It

2.13 Baize cloth (McCabe)

is normally used in its natural colour, and the term 'camel' is used to describe this shade of yellow tan.

Candlewick Traditionally used for bedspreads and warm, heavy housecoats. It is made by pulling soft, thick yarns through a base fabric and then cutting it, often into floral or geometric designs.

Canvas A heavy, strong, plain weave fabric originally made of cotton, flax or hemp but now of mixed or synthetic fibres. Canvas is available in various weights, and is used extensively in all kinds of crafts and as various forms of interfacing.

Cashmere Noted for its luxurious softness, this wool comes from the Kashmir goat. Cashmere is not durable, and is usually mixed with other fibres to prolong its life.

Cavalry twill Traditionally used for making uniforms, this fabric is very strong with a twilled diagonal rib.

Challis A soft, lightweight fabric made of wool, cotton, man-made fibres or a mixture.

Chambray A lightweight cloth of cotton alone or mixed with other fibres, where a coloured warp is woven with a white weft thread. Similar in appearance to denim but much lighter.

Cheesecloth A loosely woven, plain weave, white fabric which was originally used for making cheese. Useful in craftwork and as a fine interfacing/interlining in fashion.

Chenille A pile yarn which is knitted or woven into fuzzy or novelty fabric with an interesting pile finish.

Cheviot Made from the wool of the Cheviot sheep, this is a rough surfaced, rugged cloth primarily used as a coating.

Chiffon A sheer, light, drapable fabric which was originally made of pure silk. Today it is usually of a man-made fibre,

but pure silk chiffon is sold in the luxury market.

China silk Traditionally a lining fabric, light, soft and with a plain weave. These days, as pure silks can be so expensive, China silk is sometimes used in fashion and lingerie for reasons of economy. Also called Jap silk.

Chintz A closely woven, cotton, plain weave fabric – often printed in bright florals – with a glazed finish. Can be used in fashion, crafts and upholstery.

Ciré Usually a very slippery fabric with an extremely shiny or glossy finish.

Corded fabric Often shortened to 'cord', this fabric has a lengthwise rib – sometimes woven in stripes.

Corduroy A corded fabric where the rib has been woven or sheared, thus producing a smooth, velvet-type nap. Today made in many fibres, corduroy was traditionally made in cotton.

Cotton Cotton is both the name of the fibre from the cotton plant and the fabric made from these fibres. Varying types of cotton plants provide cotton of high or inferior quality. The name of the cotton, such as Eygptian or Indian, will often denote its quality. Today cotton is often mixed with man-made fibres for durability and/or economy.

Cotton knits Often of a finer gauge than wool or synthetic knits, a cotton knit is obtained in the same way. Traditionally a fabric for underwear, these knits are now extensively used in fashion and sportswear as well. To lessen shrinkage and add durability the cotton is often mixed with synthetic fibres.

Crash Originally linen but now made of other fibres too, this is a coarse woven fabric with a rough surface. It is used in fashion, crafts and as curtain fabric.

Crêpe A crêpe fabric has an all-over crinkled surface effect which is obtained by the area of weaving with a crêpe yarn. Crêpe yarns are obtained by giving them such a high twist that the yarn kinks. Crêpe fabrics are made in a variety of fibres, although the two most traditional are wool and silk.

Crêpe-backed satin This is a two-faced fabric – one of satin, the other of crêpe. Used extensively for bridal wear, evening wear and lingerie.

Crêpe de Chine A traditional pure silk fabric which is today imitated in man-made fabrics.

Cretonne Traditionally made of cotton in a plain or twill weave, this fabric is usually used for home furnishings and draperies.

Damask Traditionally used for table linen and home furnishings, damask is occasionally used in fashion. Usually made from linen or cotton on a jacquard loom, these fibres are now sometimes mixed with synthetics.

Denim Denim is traditionally a twill weave, hard-wearing fabric from which workers' jeans were made in the traditional blue colour. This fabric had a coloured warp and a white weft. When jeans and denim made the transition from work to fashion wear, the name of denim was given to many other imitation fabrics – cross-dyed, brushed, knits and woven.

Dobby Less elaborate than jacquard, dobby fabric has small geometric patterns incorporated into the weave, such as piqué fabric.

Donegal Although this fabric was originally woven by hand in County Donegal in Ireland, today it often is a term applied to any tweed made with thick slubs as part of the fabric. These slubs are often coloured, and the term tweed is generally used with Donegal.

Double cloth A two-faced cloth where two fabrics are woven and joined by threads in the centre. This reversible fabric is usually used for coating, and the two sides may differ in colour and/or design.

Double knit Usually a firm knit, and very stable. The fabric appears the same on both sides, with rows of fine ribs in the lengthwise direction.

Doupion A traditional silk fabric made from the yarn of two fibres of silk obtained where two silkworms have been cocooned together. This double-fibred yarn gives a fabric which is thick, uneven and irregular in texture compared with other silks. A synthetic doupion fabric is less expensive than silk.

Drill A strong, twill weave fabric used where strength is essential for overalls, uniforms and tickings.

Duck An extremely durable fabric. It can be made from many fibres. It is closely woven, heavy and either plain or a basket-type weave. Can be used in craft work and as interfacing.

Duffel cloth Today available in any colour, but traditionally the fabric in which blue and green duffel coats were made. The fabric is thick, heavy and napped.

Faille Originally made in silk but there are many excellent synthetic varieties now available. Faille has a very narrow crosswise rib which gives it a slightly heavier finish than crêpe de Chine.

Felt True felt is made from wool and hair fibres rolled and pressed together with heat and moisture: other fibres can be substituted. Felt is used mainly in craft work and millinery.

Flannel Usually wool and wool mixtures: a soft fabric with a brushed finish. However, cotton flannel is also available.

Flannelette A fairly lightweight fabric, usually cotton and brushed only on one side. Modern synthetics are sometimes mixed with the cotton to provide an ideal fabric for children's wear, shirts and nightwear.

Flax The product of the flax plant, from which linen is made.

Fleece Used to describe the wool of sheep and similar animals. It can be applied to any deep-pile synthetic fabric.

Foulard In plain or twill weave, lightweight and normally of silk, cotton or mixed fibres, this fabric was traditionally used for ties, scarves, dressing gowns and so on. Usually printed with a small all-over pattern: foulard is also used to describe this type of print.

Fur fabric/fake fur Made usually in a modacrylic fibre. Imitates animal pelts.

Fusible fabric These can be bonded to other fabrics by heat, moisture and pressure. The dots of polyamide resins on the wrong side of the fusible fabric are placed against the wrong side of the other fabric. A large variety of interfacings are available for fusing.

Gabardine Has a close twill weave and is a strong fabric for coats and suits. Wool and cotton gabardine are traditional fabrics, but almost any fibres and mixtures can be used.

Gauze A very flimsy, sheer woven fabric which is quite open in appearance. Usually of cotton or silk.

Georgette A sheer fabric, similar to chiffon but with a slightly heavier, more opaque finish because it is made with crêpe yarns. Silk, wool or synthetic fibres can be used.

Gingham Applied both to fabric and to the small checked design that is usually woven into the fabric, although plaid ginghams are also produced. A plain weave fabric with the design woven into it by the use of various coloured yarns. Made in cotton or cotton mixtures.

Grosgrain A heavy ribbed fabric, usually made in narrow widths and used as ribbon: wider versions can be used for academic gowns. Grosgrain can be made from a variety of fibres.

Harris tweed A hairy tweed, hand woven on the Outer Hebrides. Used for coats and suits.

Herringbone A twill weave where the weave reverses so that the twill pattern creates the effect of the backbone of the herring. Traditionally made in wool and used for coats and suits.

Homespun This fabric has thick nubby yarns and has a rough surface, imitating the original fabrics which were made from yarns spun by hand.

Honeycomb A weave that resembles the honeycomb, with diamonds or other geometrics.

Horsehair The hair from the mane and/or tail of the horse. Used to create an interfacing for stiffening and strength. These days other fibres – such as goat or man-made – are often used.

Illusion Usually made of silk or nylon, this is a very fine veiling fabric.

Interfacing A stiffening or supporting fabric used to give additional body and strength. Used in fashion garments in such places as collars, cuffs, pocket flaps and front edges. Also used in crafts and upholstery for support of fabric and/or stitching or for stiffening.

Interlining Should not be confused with interfacing, underlining or lining. Interlining is an additional layer of fabric placed between the top fabric and lining to provide extra warmth. Applies to coats and jackets and also curtains.

Jacquard A term used to describe an intricate woven or knitted pattern.

Jap silk Another name for China silk.

Jersey Technically this is a knit fabric with plain stitches on the right side and purl stitches on the wrong – as in hand knitting. Many other types of soft knitted fabrics are given this title, however.

2.14 Gingham (McCabe)

Khaki Applies both to the earth/olive green colour and to the classic uniforms made from the variety of fabrics under this heading.

Knit Knitting is the method of forming a fabric by stringing rows of loops to rows of loops in preceding and succeeding rows. There are a variety of knit fabrics in production in almost all types of yarns and fibres for every conceivable use.

Lace A decorative, fine, open fabric of linen, cotton, silk, wool or synthetic fibres or mixtures of these. The lace pattern can be made with or without a background fabric of net. There are a number of types of lace:

All-over The pattern covers the entire piece of wide fabric and is not an isolated pattern on a background net.

Ajour A very open design scattered across the background.

Alençon The solid design is outlined by a cord. Made on a sheer net fabric. The cord gives definition to the design and makes the lace slightly heavier in weight.

Antique When made on a machine, this is usually used for curtaining. It is a heavy lace made on square, knotted net and with the design darned on to the net. Originally this type of lace was handmade.

Argentan Similar to Alençon, but the design is usually larger and the motif not outlined with the cord.

Battenberg Formed by tape or braid joined by bars.

Beading An openwork lace which has holes through which to thread ribbon.

Belgian Any lace made in Belgium.

Binche Handmade motifs are applied to a machine-made background net. Originated in Belgium.

Bobbin Handmade on a pillow with pins holding the yarns in position, which create the designs.

Bourdon Made on a machine where the design (normally of scrolls) is outlined with a heavy thread.

Breton Named after the area of France where it originated. Made with heavy, often brightly coloured yarns embroidered on to a background of open net.

Brussels Applies to a variety of laces from Brussels, which can be either bobbin or needlepoint in design.

Chantilly Has the design outlined by thick cord, and is a popular bridal fabric. It is a bobbin lace.

Cluny Also a bobbin lace. Made with thick cotton, which gives it a very heavy appearance.

Crochet Made by hand with the crochet hook, and usually used as motifs or edging laces.

Hairpin Worked over a hairpin or hairpin-shaped tool to provide a delicate, narrow lace.

Irish Applied to all laces made in Ireland, whether by crochet or by the embroidered net method.

Needlepoint Made with a sewing or embroidery needle. Buttonhole stitches are the basis for the design.

Nottingham A term applied to most machine-made laces. Nottingham was one of the first places to make lace by a machine method.

Valenciennes A very rich lace which originated in France in the seventeenth century. It is a flat bobbin lace made with one thread.

Venetian A needlepoint lace with a floral pattern and connected by picot edging.

Lambswool Describes the wool taken from the lamb before it is seven months old. It is very soft and luxurious.

Lamé A very glittery fabric made with metallic yarns or a mixture of mainly metallic and some other fibres. It can be woven or knitted.

Lawn A very lightweight fabric, originally made from linen but more commonly now made in cotton and cotton and synthetic mixtures. It has a plain weave and can be used in fashion, lingerie and crafts.

Leather The hide on any animal with the fur removed. Various types of leathers can be used for dress and craft work.

Leatherette Any imitation leather.

Linen One of the oldest fabrics known to man, linen is made from flax. It is woven into many fabrics of different weight and is often now mixed with synthetic fibres to increase its resistance to creasing. Linen is used in fashion and crafts.

Lining A general term for any fabric made in the same shape as the outer one, in fashion, crafts and household items. Lining is there to support, and to protect and hide seams and darts.

Loden A cloth of similar construction and weight to duffel cloth.

Man-made fibres/fabrics Refers to all fibres which are not of natural origin – including things like acetate which comes from cellulose. Synthetic fibres are those originating wholly from the laboratory such as polyester which is made from petroleum.

Matte Denotes a dull finish on a fabric.

Melton This cloth is very densely woven, with only a slight nap and a very smooth appearance. Used extensively for overcoats and uniforms.

Mohair The long, lustrous hair of the Angora goat. It can be used by itself as a luxury yarn in knit and woven cloth, but is extensively mixed with other fibres for suitings and coatings.

Moiré The finish given to a fabric – often taffeta – which produces a distinctive 'watermarked' effect.

Moss crêpe Refers to any crêpe fabric that has a moss-like finish, although originally this effect was created with a dobby weave and viscose yarn.

Mousseline A large variety of fairly sheer, lightweight fabrics in any pure and man-made fibre. It is quite crisp.

Mousseline de soie Pure silk, light, sheer, plain weave and similar to chiffon.

Muslin A plain weave fabric of various weights woven from cotton or cotton mixture. It can be used in fashion and crafts and also household items. Muslin is useful as an interfacing medium and for making toiles.

Nap Applied to the surface of a cloth if it is raised, cut and smoothed in a certain direction. A pile is also referred to as a nap – as with a velvet, plush or cord. Care must be taken when cutting out such fabrics to ensure that all the pieces are cut the same way up, or else shading will occur.

Net Either made by machine or knotted by hand, and is an open fabric with geometrically shaped holes. It can be made from very many fibres to produce delicate nets for bridal veils, through to very heavy nets for draperies and craft uses.

2.15 Linen (McCabe)

Novelty Used extensively in the trade to describe any fabric with unusual colouring, design, weave, texture and so on.

Nun's veiling Traditionally made of wool, this is a plain weave, often quite sheer fabric used for nuns' habits and made in black or white. It is now made of woollen, worsted or man-made fibres and used as a fashion fabric.

Nylon Nylon was the very first man-made fibre to be produced, and is made from petroleum. It has great toughness, lightness and durability, and resists moths and mildew. It is used for an amazing variety of fabrics to make anything from nylon stockings and tights to overalls and mosquito netting! It is also often used mixed with other fibres.

Oilcloth Any fabric treated with oil to make it waterproof. Oilskin was originally a term for oilcloth used in making raincoats, but today it covers a variety of waterproof coating fabrics, particularly those with a synthetic coating on the right side of the fabric.

Organdie/organza Originally organdie was made from cotton and organza from silk. Both were very sheer, lightweight fabrics similar to chiffon but crisper. Today the terms are synonymous, and the fabric is made from polyster fibres as well as the traditional natural ones.

Ottoman Similar to faille, this fabric has wider, horizontal ribs and is usually produced in wool, silk, mixtures and/or man-made fibres.

Peau de soie A satin weave, closely woven, soft fabric with a soft lustre, rather heavy in weight. It is used particularly for formal wear and wedding gowns. Originally made in pure silk, it is often copied in polyester, when it is called just peau.

Petersham A very similar ribbon to grosgrain, but usually slightly stiffer.

Picot A picot trim is a series of small loops along the edge of a fabric when manufactured or crocheted or hand embroidered. This technique can be copied on many of the top sewing machines and is most effective. Picot trimming may also be purchased by the yard or metre.

Piqué White piqué is a classic fabric for white collars and cuffs. The fabric is woven with small, raised geometric patterns. Traditionally a cotton fabric, it is often now made with a blend of cotton and synthetic fibres.

Plissé Plissé should not be confused with seersucker, as the puckering which is a feature of both fabrics is obtained in different ways. Plissé is obtained by printing a plain cotton fabric with a chemical solution; this area shrinks, causing the unprinted area to pucker. The puckering is permanent, but the fabric should not be ironed.

Polyester Probably the most widely used of the man-made fibres. Modern technology has invented techniques whereby a polyester fabric can closely resemble an amazingly large number of fabric types of all thicknesses. Polyester can be used alone or mixed with other fibres.

Poodle cloth Can be woven or knitted. It is a heavy cloth with surface loops that resemble the coat of the poodle.

Poplin With a fine horizontal rib, this fabric is usually made of cotton or cotton mixtures. It is slightly heavier and crisper than lawn.

Rabbit hair The hair of the rabbit is not used alone but, combined with other fibres, it can give a soft and interesting texture to woven or knitted fabrics.

Sailcloth Originally a firmly woven cotton canvas used for sails. It is now of cotton and man-made fibres. This fabric can be used in fashion and crafts and for interfacings. Canvas, duck and sailcloth are all used interchangably.

Sateen This strong and lustrous fabric is usually made of cotton and has a satin weave. The name differentiates it from satin weave fabrics made of silk or polyester.

Satin Satin woven fabrics are usually made of silk or polyester, and various types have developed.

Antique satin Used primarily in furnishing for drapes and curtains, this satin is double faced: one side is lustrous satin, the other has a slubbed look.

Crêpe-backed satin Another double-faced fabric, with one side lustrous satin and the other a crêpe finish.

Double-faced satin This satin has two sides of lustrous satin finish.

Duchesse satin With a lustrous satin finish on the right side, this is a heavy and important fabric often used for wedding gowns and evening wear.

Slipper satin Lighter in weight than duchesse satin, but also with a lustrous finish on the right side only. It is used for many purposes in fashion and crafts and for making evening shoes.

Sea Island cotton This cotton has the longest and finest fibres and is used only in the highest-quality cotton fabric.

Seersucker Normally made from cotton and/or cotton blends, this fabric has a permanent puckered effect in alternating stripes obtained by altering the tension on groups of yarns whilst weaving. Seersucker should not be confused with plissé.

Serge A traditionally hard-wearing woollen cloth for suits and coats made with a twill weave. Today other fibres can be used.

Shantung This fabric was traditionally made of silk in a plain weave but with slubs providing a textured effect. Silk shantung is still available, but there are excellent man-made fibre alternatives.

Shirting Applied to almost any fabric suitable for making shirts, including cottons, crêpes and satins.

Silk The only natural continuous filament fibre. It is produced by the silkworm. Silk has always been a luxury fabric. There are many types of silk and silk fabric, and the names are often used for modern synthetic replacements.

Suiting Any fabric that will tailor well, take a sharp crease and is of a suitable weight for suit or jacket making. It should be durable and crease resistant.

Sweatshirting A knitted fabric with a smooth face and a fleecy backing. Used primarily for sports clothes, it is now being adopted for many items of leisure wear. Originally this fabric was made of cotton, but now it is often made from acrylic yarns.

Taffeta Originally a pure silk fabric of plain weave, with a crisp finish and shiny surface. Taffetas are now often made in acetate. Various types are available:

Antique taffeta An exceptionally stiff fabric resembling those of the eighteenth century. It often has an iridescent effect.

Faille taffeta Has a prominent rib as in faille.

Moiré taffeta Has the moiré (watermark) finish and is usually crisp and luxurious.

Paper taffeta Very lightweight and very crisp.

Terry cloth A very absorbent cloth made of cotton or cotton mixtures with a looped pile on one or both sides of the cloth. It is primarily used for towels, but also used for leisure and sportswear.

Thai silk This silk fabric is made in Thailand. It is usually heavy, slubbed and very highly coloured or iridescent.

Ticking Applies to all heavy, twill weave fabrics which are featherproof, although today pillows and cushions are often stuffed with man-made fillings. Ticking is also used to cover mattresses, and traditional ticking was usually in a woven stipe of white and black.

Tulle Originally tulle was an extremely fine net made of silk, but it has come to be made in nylon and other man-made fibres. It is a traditional fabric for bridal veils.

Tussah silk A silk fabric woven from the silk from uncultivated worms. It has a rougher texture than cultivated silk, and has a tan colour which cannot be bleached.

Tweed Traditionally a woollen fabric, it is now sometimes mixed with man-made fibres. It is a woven cloth with characteristic coloured slubs of yarn, and the surface is usually somewhat hairy. Donegal, Harris, Irish and Scottish are the main tweeds.

Velour Can be a knit or woven fabric with a short, cut pile. Terry velour looks rich but has not the drying properties of normal terry. Polyster velours are used extensively for leisure and sportswear.

Velvet Made by one of two methods, velvet has a short, cut, dense pile. Original velvets were of silk, but later became made in cotton. Other fibres are now used, including nylon. Some velvets are made by weaving the yarn over wires thus forming the pile. When the wires are removed the pile is trimmed to the required length. The other method involves two layers of fabric being woven with long threads joining them: after weaving, the centre threads are cut to make two pieces of velvet.

Beaded velvet Another name for cut velvet

Cisele velvet A satin weave fabric with the velvet design woven in – similar to a flocked pattern.

Façonné velvet Obtained with a burn-out method of printing.

Lyons velvet Originally from France and made in silk, this velvet is very thick and somewhat stiff with a very short pile. Today it is made of man-made fibres and is used mainly for fashion and home furnishings.

Mirror velvet Has the pile pressed flat in one or more directions, which gives a shimmering finish.

Nacré velvet Has a changeable appearance, as it is made with one colour for the pile and another for the background fabric.

Panne velvet Has the pile flattened in one direction.

Uncut velvet Made by the wire method, this velvet does not have the loops cut when the fabric weaving is completed.

Velveteen Similar to corduroy, but the pile on the velveteen covers the whole surface and is thicker than the pile on cord. The difference between velvet and velveteen is that the pile on velvet is made from warp threads but the pile in velveteen is made with the filling threads. The two terms originated when velvet was made exclusively of silk and velveteen from cotton or other fibres.

Vicuna The hair from the vicuna, a type of llama from the Andes. It is traditionally one of the most expensive and luxurious of wools, but because it is hard to dye it is normally used in its natural colour of light brown.

Voile A very light fabric with a plain weave. Usually made in cotton, although now there are synthetic copies and sometimes synthetic fibres mixed with cotton. It is a delightful summer fabric for fashion garments, but is also used in home furnishings.

Waterproof fabric Any fabric which will not permit water to penetrate it.

Water-repellant fabric A fabric which repels water but will not entirely prevent penetration of the water: it is showerproof.

Wet-look fabric Any extremely shiny fabric.

Whipcord Resembling gabardine, this fabric is twilled and heavy in weight. Generally made in wool worsted, but can also be found in cotton and man-made fibres. Often used for uniforms and riding clothes.

Wool The fleecy fibres from the sheep, but similar fibres form Angora and Kashmir goats and the vicuna are also classed as wool. Wool has a natural felting ability, whereas hair and fur do not.

Woollen A fabric made from pure wool fibres, with a slightly fluffy, matt finish. It holds creases well, and may also have a nap.

Worsted Woollen yarns are carded: worsted yarns are both carded and combed to eliminate the short fibres and impurities, so that a smoother yarn results. On weaving, the fabric has a clean, smooth surface, and worsteds are more durable than normal woollens.

Zibeline A heavily napped coating with the nap pressed in one direction. It is often a mixture of fibres such as mohair, camel and wool or man-made.

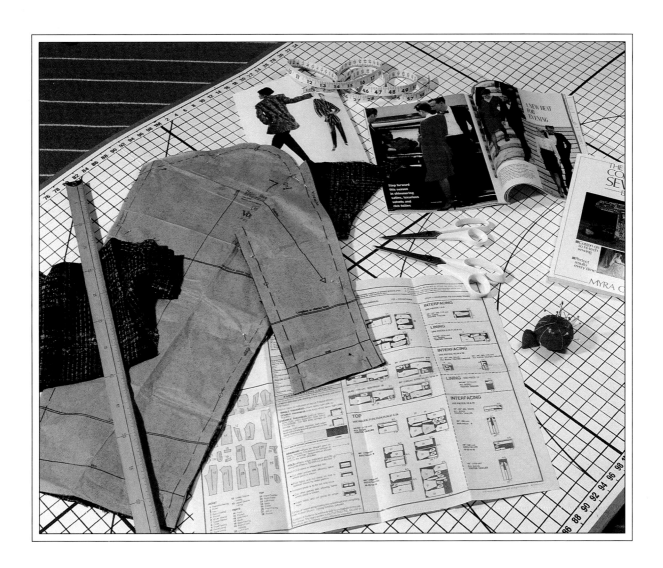

PAPER PATTERNS

The majority of dressmakers will purchase a paper pattern to the design of their choice rather than go through the long process of cutting their own pattern, which is a skilled operation.

Ladies' fashion is probably the most popular area of home sewing. However, in the catalogues (usually at the back) a large selection of patterns for children's wear, babywear and menswear will be discovered, together with toys, crafts, soft upholstery, drapes, cushions and so on.

Purchasing the fabric and pattern go hand in hand, and it is a personal choice as to which you actually buy first. Looking through the catalogue and selecting the outfit you desire is usually a pleasure, but knowing whether or not a new fashion will suit your figure type is not always easy. If in doubt, try on the new style or fashion in a ready-to-wear shop first to test it out on your own figure shape; then select your pattern!

Do not just look at the sketches or photographs in the catalogues: also read the descriptions alongside the pattern information, as these will give more detailed notes on the cut and fit of the design.

SELECTING PATTERNS

The most daunting task is usually getting the right size of pattern: a lot of mistakes can be made at this time if the correct measurements have not been taken. There are three steps to determining your correct paper pattern size, and if you follow these you will ensure success. *Do not buy the same size pattern as a ready-to-wear garment:* you must buy by comparing your own body measurements with the actual body measurements listed on the pattern company's charts. The three steps are: body measurement; figure selection; and pattern selection.

◆ BODY MEASUREMENT

Only basic body measurements are needed to determine your pattern type and size. Remember to wear proper undergarments and shoes when measuring. Also, make sure the tape measure is held snugly and firmly (not tightly) against your body, and is always parallel to the floor for circumference measurements. Take your measurements often so you are aware of any changes: precise measurements are the first step toward a perfect fit!

Misses and misses petite

◇ *Bust* Measure around the body over the fullest part of the bust and straight across the back.
◇ *Chest* Measure around the body, directly under the arms and across the top of the breasts.
◇ *Hip* Measure around the body at the fullest part – usually 18–23 cm (7–9 in) below the waist.
◇ *Back waist length* Measure from the top of the most prominent bone at the base of the neck to the natural waistline.
◇ *Height* Measure (without shoes) standing against a wall.

Toddlers, children and girls

◇ *Breast* Measure around the fullest part of the chest and straight across the back.

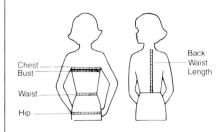

3.1 Measurements for misses and misses petite

◇ *Waist* Measure around the body at the natural waistline.
◇ *Hip* Measure across hip bones or at the fullest part (for girls).
◇ *Back waist length* Measure from the top of the most prominent bone at the base of the neck to the natural waistline.
◇ *Height* Measure child (without shoes) standing against a wall.

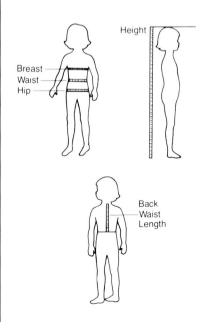

3.2 Measurements for children and girls

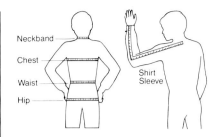

3.3 Measurements for men and boys

Men and boys

◇ *Neckband* Measure around base of neck or buy shirt pattern by ready-made size.

◇ *Chest* Measure around fullest part of chest.

◇ *Waist* Measure at natural waist over shirt.

◇ *Hip* Measure at seat or fullest part of hip.

◇ *Shirt sleeve* Measure from back base of neck across shoulder around bend of elbow to wrist.

◇ *Height* Measure (without shoes) standing against a wall.

◆ FIGURE TYPE SELECTION

Figure type is determined by your body type and your body proportions. Use the measurement charts and your height and back waist length measurements to determine your figure type.

◆ PATTERN SIZE SELECTION

Refer again to the measurement chart, and select the size in your figure type with bust, waist and hip measurements closest to your own. As your body measurements may not correspond exactly with all the measurements for one size, here are some tips to help make your size selection a little easier.

◇ *Dresses, blouses, tops, vests, jackets and coats* Select the pattern size to correspond with your bust/chest measurement. Adjust the waist and/or hip measurement if necessary.

◇ *Skirts, pants, shorts, culottes* Select the pattern size to correspond

◆ MEASUREMENT CHARTS – METRIC ◆

MISSES 'Misses' patterns are designed for a well proportioned, and developed figure: about 1.65 m to 1.68 m without shoes. Measure your Chest just above the Bust, directly under the arms

Size	Petite		Small		Medium		Large			Extra Large		XX Large	
	2	4	6	8	10	12	14	16	18	20	22	24	
Bust	72	75	78	80	63	87	92	97	102	107	112	117	cm
Chest	67	70	73	75	78	81	87	92	97	102	107	112	cm
Waist	53	56	58	61	64	67	71	76	81	87	92	97	cm
Hip	77	80	83	85	88	92	97	102	107	112	117	122	cm
Bk. Wst. Lgth	38	38.5	39.5	40	40.5	41.5	42	42.5	43	44	44.5	46	cm

MISSES PETITE This new size range is designed for the shorter Miss figure: about 1.57 m to 1.63 m without shoes.

Size	Petite	Small		Medium		Large		
	6	8	10	12	14	16	18	
Bust	78	80	83	87	92	97	102	cm
Waist	60	62	65	69	73	78	83	cm
Hip	83	85	88	92	97	102	107	cm
Back Waist Length	37	37.5	38	39	39.5	40	40.5	cm

CHILDREN'S MEASUREMENTS Measure around the breast, but not too snugly. Toddler patterns are designed for a figure between that of a baby and child. Toddlers dresses are shorter than the similar child's dress and toddler's pants have a diaper allowance

INFANTS Infants sizes are for babies who are not yet walking.

Size	Newborn	Small	Medium	Large	X-Large
Weight	6 kg max.	6–8	8–10	10–11	12–13
Height	61 cm max.	64–66	69–71	74–76	79–81

TODDLERS'

Size	Extra Small	Small		Medium	
	½	1	2	3	4
Breast or Chest	48	51	53	56	58 cm
Waist	48	50	51	52	53 cm
Approx. Height	71	79	87	94	122 cm

CHILDREN'S

Size	Extra Small	Small		Medium	Large
	2	3	4	5	6	6X
Breast or Chest	53	56	58	61	64	65 cm
Waist	51	52	53	55	56	57 cm
Hip	–	–	61	64	66	67 cm
Back Waist Length	22	23	24	25.5	27	27.5 cm
Approx. Height	89	97	104	112	119	122 cm

GIRLS' Girls' patterns are designed for the girl who has not yet begun to mature. See chart below for approximate heights without shoes.

Size	Small	Medium		Large	
	7	8	10	12	14
Breast	66	69	73	76	81 cm
Waist	58	60	62	65	67 cm
Hip	69	71	76	81	87 cm
Back Waist Length	29.5	31	32.5	34.5	36 cm
Approx. Height	127	132	142	149	155 cm

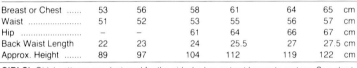

BOYS' AND TEEN BOYS' There size ranges are for growing boys and young men who have not yet reached full adult stature.

Size	BOYS Small	Medium		Large	Small	TEEN BOYS Medium		Large
	7	8	10	12	14	16	18	20
Chest	66	69	71	76	81	85	89	93 cm
Waist	58	61	64	66	69	71	74	76 cm
Hip (Seat)	69	71	75	79	83	87	90	94 cm
Neckband	30	31	32	33	34.5	35.5	37	38 cm
Approx. Height	122	127	137	147	155	163	168	173 cm
Shirt Steeve	56	58.5	63.5	66	73.5	76	78.5	81 cm

NOTE For Toddlers and Little Boys (1 to 6) – see Toddlers' and Children's charts

MEN'S Men's patterns are sized for men of average build about 1.78 m without shoes.

Size	Extra Small		Small		Medium		Large		Extra Large	
	30	32	34	36	38	40	42	44	46	48
Chest	76	81	87	92	99	102	107	112	117	122 cm
Waist	61	66	71	76	81	87	92	97	107	112 cm
Hip (seat)	79	84	89	94	99	104	109	114	119	124 cm
Neckband	33	34.5	35.5	37	38	39.5	40.5	42	43	44.5 cm
Shirt Sleeve	79	79	81	81	84	84	87	87	89	89 cm

◆ MEASUREMENT CHART – IMDERIAL ◆

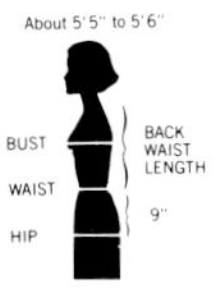

MISSES' Misses' patterns are designed for a well proportioned, and developed figure: about 5'5" to 5'6" without shoes. Measure your Chest just above the Bust, directly under the arms.

Size	Petite			Small		Medium		Large		Extra Large		XX Large
	2	4	6	8	10	12	14	16	18	20	22	24
Bust	28½	29½	30½	31½	32½	34	36	38	40	42	44	46
Chest	26½	27½	28½	29½	30½	32	34	36	38	40	42	44
Waist	21	22	23	24	25	26½	28	30	32	34	36	38
Hip	30½	31½	32½	33½	34½	36	38	40	42	44	46	48
Bk. Wst. Lgth	15	15¼	15½	15¾	16	16¼	16½	16¾	17	17¼	17½	17¾

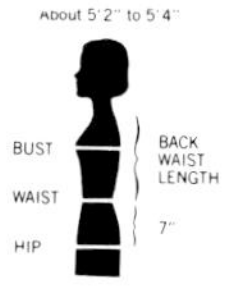

MISSES PETITE This new size range is designed for the shorter Miss figure: about 5'2" to 5'4" without shoes.

Size	Petite		Small		Medium		Large	
	6	8	10	12	14	16	18
Bust	30½	31½	32½	34	36	38	40
Waist	23½	24½	25½	27	28½	30½	32½
Hip	32½	33½	34½	36	38	40	42
Back Waist Length	14½	14¾	15	15¼	15½	15¾	16

CHILDREN'S MEASUREMENTS Measure around the breast, but not too snugly. Toddler patterns are designed for a figure between that of a baby and child. Toddlers' dresses are shorter than the similar child's dress and toddler's pants have a diaper allowance

INFANTS Infants sizes are for babies who are not yet walking.

Size	Newborn	Small	Medium	Large	X-Large
Weight	to 12 lbs.	13–17	18–21	22–25	26–29
Height	to 24 ins.	25–26	27–28	29–30	31–32

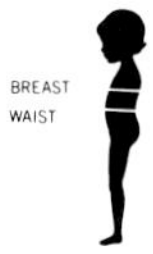

TODDLERS'

Size	Extra Small	Small		Medium	
	½	1	2	3	4
Breast or Chest	19	20	21	22	23
Waist	19	19½	20	20½	21
Approx. Height	28	31	34	37	40

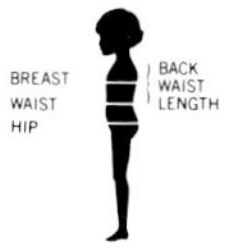

CHILDREN'S

Size	Extra Small	Small		Medium		Large
	2	3	4	5	6	6X
Breast or Chest	21	22	23	24	25	25½
Waist	20	20½	21	21½	22	22½
Hip	–	–	24	25	26	26½
Back Waist Length	8½	9	9½	10	10½	10¾
Approx. Height	35	38	41	44	47	48

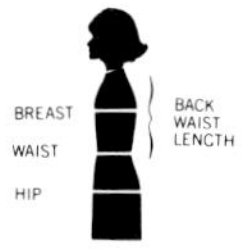

GIRLS' Girls' patterns are designed for the girl who has not yet begun to mature. See chart below for approximate heights without shoes.

Size	Small	Medium		Large	
	7	8	10	12	14
Breast	26	27	28½	30	32
Waist	23	23½	24½	25½	26½
Hip	27	28	30	32	34
Back Waist Length	11½	12½	12¾	13½	14¼
Approx. Height	50	52	56	58½	61

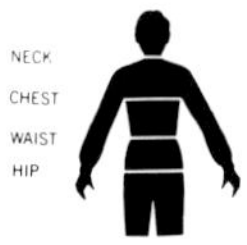

BOYS' AND TEEN BOYS' These size ranges are for growing boys and young men who have not yet reached full adult stature.

	BOYS				TEEN BOYS			
	Small	Medium		Large	Small	Medium		Large
Size	7	8	10	12	14	16	18	20
Chest	26	27	28	30	32	33½	35	36½
Waist	23	24	25	26	27	28	29	30
Hip (Seat)	27	28	29½	31	32½	34	35½	37
Neckband	11¾	12	12½	13	13½	14	14½	15
Approx. Height	48	50	54	58	61	64	66	68
Shirt Sleeve	22	23	25	26	29	30	31	32

NOTE For Toddlers and Little Boys (1 to 6) – see Toddler's and Children's charts

MEN'S Men's patterns are sized for men of average build about 5'10" without shoes.

Size	Extra Small		Small		Medium		Large		Extra Large	
	30	32	34	36	38	40	42	44	46	48
Chest	30	32	34	36	38	40	42	44	46	48
Waist	24	26	28	30	32	34	36	39	42	44
Hip (seat)	31	33	35	37	39	41	43	45	47	49
Neckband	13	13½	14	14½	15	15½	16	16½	17	17½
Shirt Sleeve	31	31	32	32	33	33	34	34	35	35

with your waist measurement and adjust the hip if necessary. If, however, your hips are very much larger than your waist, select the size closest to your hip measurement and adjust the waist.

◇ *Co-ordinate (wardrobe) patterns* These include a number of garments, such as blouse, jacket, skirt and/or trousers. Select the pattern size by your bust/chest measurement and adjust the waist and/or hips if necessary.

◇ *Between two sizes* Consider your bone structure. If you are thin and small boned, choose the smaller of the two sizes; if you are larger boned, choose the larger size. Personal preference for loose or close fit may also affect your choice of size.

◇ *Maternity patterns* Select the pattern size according to your body measurements *before* pregnancy.

Multisize patterns

These patterns are not just three sizes printed on to one pattern tissue – although they can be cut out as three individual sizes. For people with a fitting problem they can give garments of exact size. For example, if you have a size 12 bust and a size 14 hip you can cut your pattern on the size 12 cutting line for the bust, neck and shoulder area, and on the size 14 cutting line for the hip area.

Misses petite

This is designed for the shorter misses figure and proportions of design features are correctly scaled or positioned for the tiny lady (height without shoes of 1.57–1.63 m).

◆ Pattern ease

Every pattern has ease added to it: that is, extra centimetres added to the exact body measurements. *Wearing ease* is the minimum amount of ease added to allow normal body movement. *Design ease* is the extra amount of ease added to the wearing ease by the designer to create the style of each design.

◆ EASE ALLOWANCE CHART ◆

Shape of garment	Bust area			Hip area
	Dresses, blouses, shirts, tops	Jackets Lined or unlined	Coats Lined or unlined	Skirts, trousers, shorts, culottes
Close fitting	**0–2⅞ in** (0–7.3 cm)	not applicable	not applicable	not applicable
Fitted	**3–4 in** (7.5–10 cm)	**3¾–4¼ in** (9.5–10.7 cm)	**5¼–6¾ in** (13.3–17 cm)	**2–3 in** (5–7.5 cm)
Semi-fitted	**4⅛–5 in** (10.4–12.5 cm)	**4⅜–5¾ in** (11.1–14.5 cm)	**6⅞–8 in** (17.4–20.5 cm)	**3⅛–4 in** (7.9–10 cm)
Loose fitting	**5⅛–8 in** (13–20.5 cm)	**5¾–10 in** (14.5–25.5 cm)	**8⅛–12 in** (20.7–30.5 cm)	**4⅛–6 in** (10.4–15 cm)
Very loose fitting	**over 8 in** (over 20.5 cm)	**over 10 in** (over 25.5 cm)	**over 12 in** (over 30.5 cm)	**over 6 in** (over 15 cm)

Ease allowances are not applicable for stretchable knit fabrics

This is another important reason for *reading* the description on the pattern envelope or in the catalogue. If you look at a design and see that it is extremely full and flowing in style, you should not be tempted to buy a size smaller than you need 'because it is big'! The garment is designed this way, but it must still be the correct size to fit exactly on the shoulders. Similarly, if a design looks very figure hugging you should not be tempted to just buy a size up: if you do not like very fitted clothes, select another style. Buying a size up will mean that the garment will eventually be totally out of proportion for you.

Fitted, close fitting, loose fitting, semi-fitted, very loose fitting – these are terms found in the garment descriptions on pattern envelopes. Each term indicates a general amount of wearing ease and design ease that is built into the pattern. The specific amount of ease will vary from style to style.

PATTERN ENVELOPES

Everything you need to know about a pattern and what you require for making it up is detailed on the pattern envelope. On the front is shown the chosen design and the various views – usually labelled A, B, C and so on. The views may have different lengths of sleeve, lengths of skirt, necklines and other details (Figure 3.4). The instructions for all these views will be included on the sheet inside, and there will be pattern pieces for cutting fabric, linings, interfacings and so on. As well as the sketches or photograph of the design on the front of the envelope, there will be the number of the pattern and the size of the pieces, such as size 10 or multisize (12-14-16).

It is on the back of the envelope that the majority of necessary information is detailed (Figure 3.5). Sketches will show the back views of the corresponding views illustrated on the front of the envelope. These will detail design features such as zipper placement, tucks, darts, yokes and pockets. The description of the garment(s) will be brief but accurate. For instance, 'loose fitting' means that the designer intended the garment to be loose and that extra ease is included to get this effect. 'Extended shoulders' means that the shoulder line will be wider than the natural shoulder. 'Low armholes' indicates that the underarm sleeve seam will be cut low into the bodice. 'Mock bands' means that the pocket top will be turned over and top stitched, and not that a separate decorative band will be sewn to the pocket top. 'Narrow hem' is usually a narrow (⅝ in) hem that is double turned and top stitched into place. Finally, 'purchased belt' indicates that although a belt is shown on the sketch on the front of the pattern envelope, there are no instructions or pattern pieces included for a belt.

If you read these descriptions closely when you select a pattern, you will have a complete understanding of what making the garment(s) entails and also of all the design details.

Notions is an American term for haberdashery, although it is becoming more widely used in the UK. All the items listed under this heading will be required to complete the garment or outfit, and it is important to refer to the list whilst you are still in the store to ensure you have all the things you will require. Many happily planned weekends of sewing have been aborted because the sewer has omitted to buy these basic essentials – or just forgotten the zip! Thread should be included under notions – but rarely is! Buy the required thread when you purchase the fabric to ensure an exact colour match; do not wait to check on stocks at home, and do not try to carry the colour 'in your eye' when you go shopping. If you cannot get the exact match, buy the nearest shade *darker*.

The list of fabrics will indicate suitable alternatives for making the garment(s). It is important to follow these guidelines because the hang of the dress will be affected if the wrong weight is used. Clearly one would not make a winter coat in a thin cotton or an evening dress in a gabardine. However, it might not be obvious from the sketch that a dress/outfit would be better made up in a soft jersey fabric rather than a stiffer cotton, so this designer information is very welcome and should be followed.

When it states that extra fabric should be allowed to match plaids or stripes – and many patterns do – then the extra required can only be assessed at the counter when the size

of the plaid or stripe can be measured and the extra calculated. If in doubt, ask the assistant to help. Extra fabric should also be purchased to allow for matching a large pattern such as a floral or a geometric.

Nap denotes that the fabric has a one-way design. For example, all the flower heads will point in one direction; all the pieces must be cut out in that direction so that the flowers are not going upwards on some pieces and downwards on

others! Nap also applies to the pile direction on velvets and fur fabrics, and likewise to a shaded fabric.

On the chart the sizes are spread out along the top: find your size and the column underneath for the view that you are making up. On the right-hand side is the width of fabrics, and so the amount shown under your size, view and corresponding fabric width is the amount required. For example, on the illustrated envelope, if you are a size 12

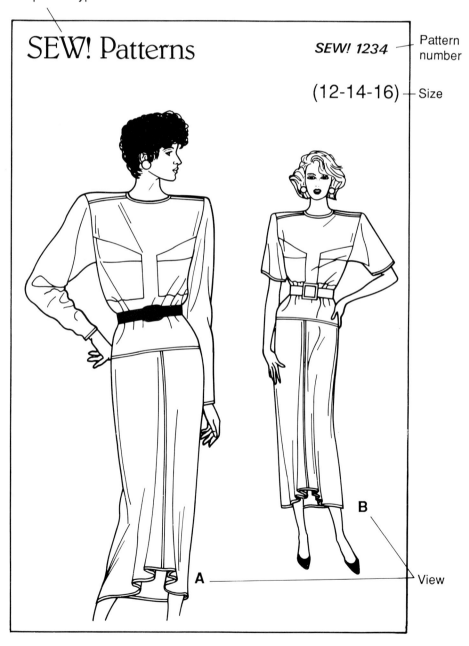

Manufacturer's name and pattern type

SEW! Patterns

SEW! 1234 — Pattern number

(12-14-16) — Size

A

B

View

3.4 Envelope front

making up view B in a fabric which is 60 inches wide, you will require 2 yards of fabric. This envelope has metric instructions alongside the imperial. If you are working in metres then, using the illustration again, for a size 12 making up view B in a 150 centimetre fabric you will require 2.2 metres.

The interfacing required is also shown. It is expensive to purchase interfacing in little pieces each time you make a new outfit. Instead, purchase a metre or two now and again so that you always have it to hand when required.

At the bottom of the chart are the widths and lengths of the garment(s). According to what is in the envelope, it will show measurements of skirts, trousers, jackets and so on. It will also show the back length of each garment, finished to the hem: measure from the little nobbly bone at the base of the neck. The width measurement is helpful to determine how full is the skirt or trouser leg. In addition, if you are considering buying a fabric of different width to that shown on the list, you will know whether you can use that width, particularly if it is a narrow one: just do a simple division sum!

On toy, craft, household and upholstery patterns the information will correspond to that on a fashion pattern. Similarly, all the notions, fabrics, interfacings and so on will be listed.

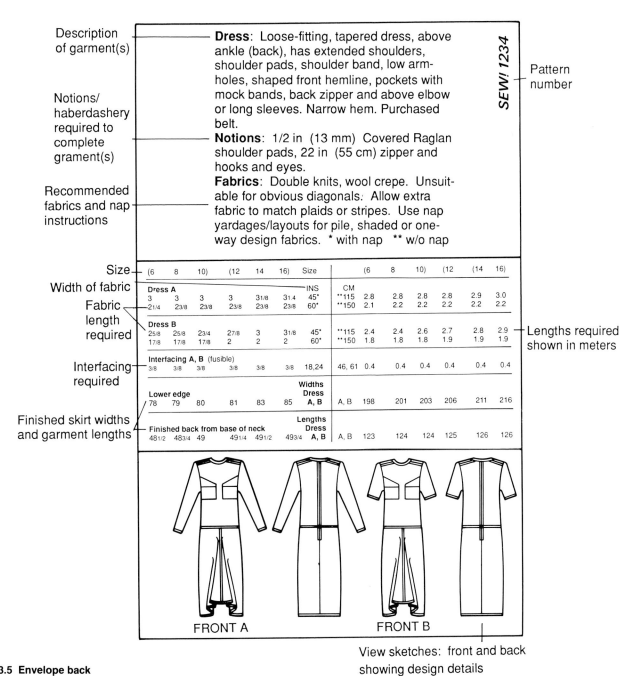

Description of garment(s)

Dress: Loose-fitting, tapered dress, above ankle (back), has extended shoulders, shoulder pads, shoulder band, low armholes, shaped front hemline, pockets with mock bands, back zipper and above elbow or long sleeves. Narrow hem. Purchased belt.

SEW! 1234 — Pattern number

Notions/haberdashery required to complete grament(s)

Notions: 1/2 in (13 mm) Covered Raglan shoulder pads, 22 in (55 cm) zipper and hooks and eyes.

Recommended fabrics and nap instructions

Fabrics: Double knits, wool crepe. Unsuitable for obvious diagonals. Allow extra fabric to match plaids or stripes. Use nap yardages/layouts for pile, shaded or one-way design fabrics. * with nap ** w/o nap

Size
Width of fabric
Fabric length required
Interfacing required
Finished skirt widths and garment lengths

Lengths required shown in meters

	(6	8	10)	(12	14	16)	Size		(6	8	10)	(12	(14	16)
Dress A							INS	CM						
45*	3	3	3	3	31/8	31.4	45*	**115	2.8	2.8	2.8	2.8	2.9	3.0
60*	21/4	23/8	23/8	23/8	23/8	23/8	60*	**150	2.1	2.2	2.2	2.2	2.2	2.2
Dress B														
45*	25/8	25/8	23/4	27/8	3	31/8	45*	**115	2.4	2.4	2.6	2.7	2.8	2.9
60*	17/8	17/8	17/8	2	2	2	60*	**150	1.8	1.8	1.8	1.9	1.9	1.9
Interfacing A, B (fusible)														
	3/8	3/8	3/8	3/8	3/8	3/8	18,24	46, 61	0.4	0.4	0.4	0.4	0.4	0.4
Lower edge							Widths Dress A, B							
	78	79	80	81	83	85	A, B	A, B	198	201	203	206	211	216
Finished back from base of neck							Lengths Dress A, B							
	481/2	483/4	49	491/4	491/2	493/4	A, B	A, B	123	124	124	125	126	126

FRONT A   FRONT B

3.5 Envelope back

View sketches: front and back showing design details

PATTERN INSTRUCTIONS

If I can give you just one piece of good advice, it is: always follow the pattern instructions!

Many inexperienced – and many experienced! – sewers ignore or throw away the instruction sheets. This really is inadvisable for a number of reasons. First, you need to know much of the initial information on the layouts. Then you need to know in what order to assemble the garment(s): this is particularly important with couture (designer) outfits, because often the way the pieces are assembled directly affects the hang or design features on the finished item. Another good reason for following the instructions is to do each sequence in the easiest possible way. The people who write the instructions take into account the range of stitches and techniques available on modern sewing machines, and they are constantly finding quicker and easier ways to do various jobs.

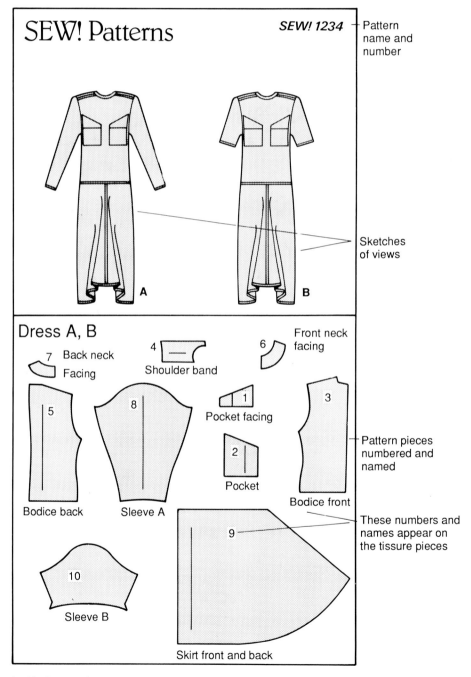

3.6 Pattern information required before sewing commences

The instruction (Figure 3.6) sheets contain two types of information:

1 Information required before sewing commences.
2 Stitching and assembly instructions.

There is always a sketch of the garment(s) and the pattern number for reference purposes.

All the pattern pieces are illustrated, numbered and named: these details correspond to the same details on the tissue pieces. The thin black lines denote grain lines. Some pieces do not have these lines because they are placed against a fold; the fold will be on the straight of grain (Figure 3.7).

◆ PREPARING THE PATTERN

These instructions will be more or less the same each time! With reference to the cutting layout, select the pieces required for the view being made and place on one side (Figures 3.7 and 3.8). To avoid confusion, refold pieces not needed and put them back in the envelope. Having separated the pieces from each other, press them with a warm, dry iron. This makes the pieces lie flatter on the fabric, and also makes the cutting out more exact. Do *not* carefully trim the surplus paper away from the edges of the pattern pieces; cutting is more accurate if you cut

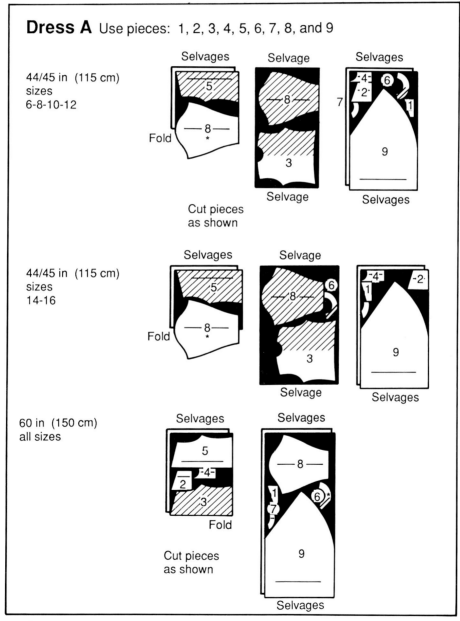

Dress A Use pieces: 1, 2, 3, 4, 5, 6, 7, 8, and 9

The heavy outline is the **cutting line**.
All seam allowances are 5/8 in (15 mm) unless otherwise indicated.
All fabric layouts are for with or without nap unless otherwise specified.

3.7 Fabric cutting layouts.

out through paper and fabric in one operation. (Cutting paper *with* the fabric in this way will not normally blunt scissors!)

At this stage check the measurements of the pieces with your own, and make all the adjustments necessary. The pieces must be adjusted *before* cutting out. There are bust, waist and hip indications on the tissue pieces to ensure accuracy. Remember when measuring pieces that ease is built in, and allow for this. If you are tall or short and need to adjust length you should alter the pieces where indicated on the adjustment lines. If you need to lengthen then slash the pieces where shown and place them over another piece of tissue; spread the amount required, and remember to keep the pieces parallel. If you need to shorten then crease the pieces along the adjustment lines, making a fold *half* the amount required.

It is always wise to check the skirt length too; if you are very tall then you may need to make it longer, and if you are short then shorter. However, if you are short and you have already folded some length out between the hip and the waist to adjust this measurement, it might be that you need to add a little to the length if your legs are longer in proportion!

Take your time over this part of the cutting-out operation, as care now is invaluable to the success of the venture; a wrongly adjusted pattern will totally ruin an outfit.

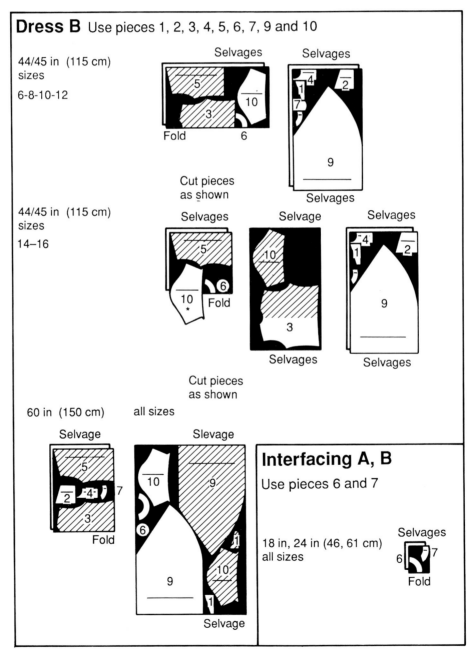

3.8 Fabric cutting layouts and interfacing A, B

◆ **LAYING OUT AND CUTTING**

With reference to the cutting layouts chart, select the size of pattern and fabric width appropriate. It is often helpful to mark the one you are to use with a felt-tip for quick reference. Note any specific instructions. In the chart illustrated, for example, it mentions that all the layouts are for fabric with or without nap. It also instructs that the heavy line is the cutting line and that the seamlines are not printed (sometimes they are). Finally, it states that all seam allowances are 5/8 in (15 mm) unless otherwise indicated.

It is wise when inexperienced to follow the cutting layout *exactly* so that you do not make mistakes. When experienced you may make minor adjustments; it is only when you know all the rules that you may occasionally break them!

The section on layout and cutting will instruct on how to interpret fabric layers and grain lines. These will vary somewhat from pattern to pattern. I always try to do a with-nap layout: that is, I always lay the pieces going in the same direction. Even when a fabric is plain and *seems* to have no shading or nap whilst in the piece, it can sometimes shade when made up. However, if for economy of fabric you need to turn pieces up the other way, this is perfectly permissible if the main nap rules are followed.

It is useful to get into the general habit of placing the right side of the fabric *up* when cutting out a single thickness, and folding right sides *inside* when cutting out a double thickness. If you require a double thickness *without* a fold then, with right sides together, fold the fabric *crosswise* and cut along the fold from selvage to selvage. Keeping right sides together, turn the upper layer completely around so that the nap runs in the same direction on both pieces.

The code for reference through the cutting and sewing instructions is illustrated in the boxes. Again it is usual for the right side of the pattern to be shown as plain white, the wrong side of the pattern as diagonal black-and-white stripes, and the fabric as plain black.

The symbols on pattern pieces are illustrated and fully explained (Figure 3.9). Two important symbols – grain line and fold line – must be taken into account at this early stage. When you lay out your pieces, the grain line must be on the straight of grain, that is exactly parallel with the selvages. On with-nap layouts, the arrows should all be pointing in the same direction. The fold line must be exactly along the fold of the fabric, and you must *never* cut along this line.

Occasionally a pattern piece is shown half white and half striped. This means that you should place it on the fabric but cut the other pieces first. When this is done, fold the fabric and cut the piece on the fold indicated by the white portion.

Sometimes a piece is to be cut only once. Lay the piece as indicated on the layout, but again cut out the other pieces first. Open out the fabric and cut the piece on a single layer.

When cutting out use long-bladed cutting-out scissors or shears. Take long, even strokes, cutting through tissue and fabric together.

If you are going to cut notches, then cut them *outside* the cutting line. Never cut them inwards or nick inside the seam allowance. Personally I prefer to use another method of marking these and other symbols.

◆ **MARKING THE PIECES AND SYMBOLS**

It is most important to mark the fabric pieces where various symbols are shown on the pattern tissue. These lines and symbols show all the construction points, and these are as important to the making up of the garment as construction points are in geometry (Figure 3.10). There are no short cuts: if you are

---

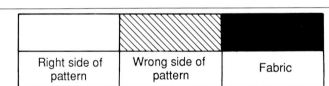

Right side of pattern	Wrong side of pattern	Fabric

Place pattern pieces on fabric according to the following:

Grainline Place on straight grain of fabric, keeping line parallel to selvage or fold. On 'with nap' layouts arrows should point in the same direction.

Fold Place edge indicated exactly along fold of fabric. *Never* cut on this line.

When **fold** piece is shown like this cut

other pieces first, allowing fabric where piece is shown.

Fold fabric and cut piece on fold in position shown by white portion.

★ indicates piece is to be cut only once. Cut other pieces first allowing fabric where piece is shown. Open fabric and cut piece on single layer.

Cut out all pieces along cutting line (solid black line) using long, even scissor strokes, cutting notches outward.

3.9 Symbols on pattern pieces

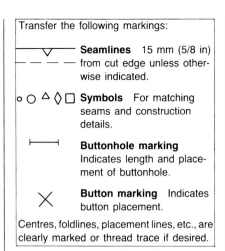

Transfer the following markings:

Seamlines 15 mm (5/8 in) from cut edge unless otherwise indicated.

Symbols For matching seams and construction details.

Buttonhole marking Indicates length and placement of buttonhole.

Button marking Indicates button placement.

Centres, foldlines, placement lines, etc., are clearly marked or thread trace if desired.

3.10 Symbols for marking fabrics

to achieve a perfectly matching garment, then the fabric pieces must be marked correctly.

There are various ways to mark, and some of the most popular methods are listed in Part 4 on haberdashery. The traditional tailor's tacks are often abandoned in favour of chalk, vanishing pen and tracing wheel, and in many inst-ances these methods are sufficient and effective. Tailor's tacks and thread tracing are, however, necessary and probably easiest when using very thick fabrics, and for tailored and semi-tailored outfits.

Seamlines are usually printed on the pattern as a broken line 5/8 in inside the cutting line. It is not always necessary to mark the whole length of the seamlines, but I advise marking where seams cross over as these are useful construction or matching points.

Symbols are usually a variety of squares, circles, triangles and diamonds, either outlined or solid. You will find a matching symbol on another piece of pattern for each one printed. For example, skirt backs will be matched up with the same symbol (probably three solid triangles); where two sleeve seams join, there will be matching symbols. Likewise, if there is a gathered skirt to fit on to a bodice there will be matching symbols: dots where the gathers end will have corresponding dots, and there will probably also be triangle shapes to match as well. Sometimes the triangles are also numbered to assist you. Dots will also be used for pocket positioning and other fashion details. In fact, any time anything is positioned, placed or joined, some sort of mark will tell you where to put it!

Buttonholes are always marked with a ├─┤ for the recommended length. However, *do not make the buttonhole this size before you purchase your buttons.* Purchase your buttons first, and then make the holes the size corresponding to your purchase! A large X usually denotes the position of the button.

Centres, fold lines and so on should be marked by a thread line, chalk or a vanishing pen. Take care if you are using tracing carbon: it is usually indelible and can irretrievably damage the cloth, and indeed if the cloth is very fine or sheer it will be clearly seen on the right side.

INFORMATION FOR SEWING AND CONSTRUCTION

◆ SEWING INFORMATION

Very brief guidelines are given for sewing on the instruction sheet (Figure 3.11). For full details refer to the appropriate parts of this book. For hand sewing techniques refer to a suitable textbook.

Because the sheets are printed in black and white, a shading key is necessary to interpret the right and wrong sides of pattern pieces, fabrics, lining and interfacings.

Basting is the American term for tacking, and it is commonly used now in the UK to denote this technique in both hand and machine stitching. Seams should *always* be tacked or pinned before sewing together, as should any other detail such as darts, tucks and zippers. Do not be tempted to just throw the two layers of fabric under the machine without anchoring them together, as stretching or mismatching of pieces can occur. Tips will be found in Part 5.

Pressing is most important: it is

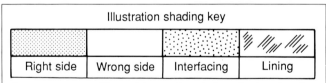

Illustration shading key

Right side	Wrong side	Interfacing	Lining

Baste seams, matching notches and symbols, using long hand or machine stitching or pins.

Stitch seams in direction of fabric grain to prevent stretching (generally from widest to narrowest part of each piece).

Press as you sew. Press seams flat, then press open, unless otherwise instructed.

- Remove visible basting stitches.
- Press straight seams on a flat surface.
- Press curved seams over a rounded surface.

Clip seam allowances where necessary so they will lie flat.

3.11 Sewing information

essential to press each piece of fabric each time it is stitched. Full details on pressing and equipment will be found in Parts 1 and 5.

The information sheet will also detail the sewing terms and techniques that are used for the garment construction. These will obviously vary from pattern to pattern, although some techniques will be used for virtually every outfit.

Many stitches and techniques are detailed in Part 5.

◆ **MAKING UP THE OUTFIT OR GARMENT**

Having digested all the pattern information, and altered, cut out and marked up, you are ready to put the garment together! Follow the instructions step by step as illustrated,

and if you do not know the stitch or technique listed then refer to your sewing book for more details (Figure 3.12). However, a prestige pattern will have very comprehensive details and instructions included. Do not be tempted to cut corners, because in the long run it is quicker to do something correctly than to have to unpick and do it again.

I find that putting the pieces

Dress A

Step 1 – Bodice

Turn in 1/4 in (6 mm) on upper edge of *pocket facing* 1; press.

With right sides together, pin pocket facing to *pocket* 2 at upper edge. Stitch long edge and ends. Trim.

Turn pocket facing to inside, turning in remaining seam allowances and diagonally folding corners, as shown. Press.

Baste close to inner pressed edge.

Topstitch along basting through all thicknesses.

Pin pocket to *bodice front* 3, matching symbols. *Edgestitch* along edges, as shown.

3.12 Part of pattern instructions for assembling the garment

together on a padded ironing board – rather than a slippery table surface – is helpful, especially as you can temporarily pin down into the surface of the board to hold the pieces where you want them. Pinning pleats and tucks this way is particularly helpful, as you can press them in place *before* removing them from the board, knowing that they are correctly placed.

Another tip is to remove the pattern tissue from each piece *only* as you come to use it! If after cutting out and marking up you strip all the tissue off of the fabric pieces, you lose a lot of helpful information.

Pin the instruction sheet on a board adjacent to where you are working, because you need to refer to it constantly. Also, keep the pattern pieces out throughout the making up, so that you can refer to them easily to recheck a detail or measurement.

Note: in this section a fashion pattern has been used as illustration – the same basic rules will apply to craft and home furnishing patterns.

METRIC EQUIVALENCY TABLES

◆ INCHES INTO MILLIMETRES AND CENTIMETRES ◆
(Slightly rounded for your convenience)

inches	mm	cm	inches	cm	inches	cm
⅛	3	–	7	18	29	73.5
¼	6	–	8	20.5	30	76
⅜	10	1	9	23	31	78.5
½	13	1.3	10	25.5	32	81.5
⅝	15	1.5	11	28	33	84
¾	20	2	12	30.5	34	86.5
⅞	22	2.2	13	33	35	89
1	25	2.5	14	35.5	36	91.5
1¼	32	3.2	15	38	37	94
1½	38	3.8	16	40.5	38	96.5
1¾	45	4.5	17	43	39	99
2	50	5	18	46	40	102
2½	65	6.3	19	48.5	41	104
3	75	7.5	20	51	42	107
3½	90	9	21	53.5	43	109
4	100	10	22	56	44	112
4½	115	11.5	23	58.5	45	115
5	125	12.5	24	61	46	117
5½	140	14	25	63.5	47	120
6	150	15	26	66	48	122
			27	68.5	49	125
			28	71	50	127

◆ YARDS TO METRES ◆
(Slightly rounded for your convenience)

Yards	Metres	Yards	Metres	Yards	Metres	Yards	Metres	Yards	Metres
⅛	0.15	2⅛	1.95	4⅛	3.80	6⅛	5.60	8⅛	7.45
¼	0.25	2¼	2.10	4¼	3.90	6¼	5.75	8¼	7.55
⅜	0.35	2⅜	2.20	4⅜	4.00	6⅜	5.85	8⅜	7.70
½	0.50	2½	2.30	4½	4.15	6½	5.95	8½	7.80
⅝	0.60	2⅝	2.40	4⅝	4.25	6⅝	6.10	8⅝	7.90
¾	0.70	2¾	2.55	4¾	4.35	6¾	6.20	8¾	8.00
⅞	0.80	2⅞	2.65	4⅞	4.50	6⅞	6.30	8⅞	8.15
1	0.95	3	2.75	5	4.60	7	6.40	9	8.25
1⅛	1.05	3⅛	2.90	5⅛	4.70	7⅛	6.55	9⅛	8.35
1¼	1.15	3¼	3.00	5¼	4.80	7¼	6.65	9¼	8.50
1⅜	1.30	3⅜	3.10	5⅜	4.95	7⅜	6.75	9⅜	8.60
1½	1.40	3½	3.20	5½	5.05	7½	6.90	9½	8.70
1⅝	1.50	3⅝	3.35	5⅝	5.15	7⅝	7.00	9⅝	8.80
1¾	1.60	3¾	3.45	5¾	5.30	7¾	7.10	9¾	8.95
1⅞	1.75	3⅞	3.55	5⅞	5.40	7⅞	7.20	9⅞	9.05
2	1.85	4	3.70	6	5.50	8	7.35	10	9.15

HABERDASHERY

A myriad of notions contribute to our stitching and sewing needs, be it fashion, crafts, toys, household or repairs. Some are traditional; some have been developed in a computer-oriented world.

Working or material haberdashery – as opposed to equipment purchased in the haberdashery department – includes:

◇ Needles and threads.

◇ Zips of all weights and types.

◇ Piping cords and decorative insertion piping strips.

◇ Ribbons of every hue and width imaginable, in a variety of finishes, to be threaded, couched, appliquéd, ruched, faggotted, braided and bowed.

◇ Seam bindings and fold-over braids: bias bindings and grosgrain.

◇ Crochet threads for buttonhole cording and decorative couching.

◇ Every variety of waistbanding: Petastretch, petersham, nylon, polyester, sew-in and fusible.

◇ Curtain tapes in an amazing array of pleatings, lining tapes and tape for sheers.

◇ Teddy eyes, dolls' faces, and animal noses.

◇ Stuffing, wadding, boning and a huge variety of interfacings.

Haberdashery departments definitely need to be explored at great length!

BUCKLES

Clasp Buckle   **Slide Buckle**   **Prong Buckle**

4.1 Buckles

Buckles are available in many styles, sizes and materials. These include wood, plastic, metal, bone, and fabric covered. Popular kits provide the basic buckle and instructions for covering with your own fabric. There are three main types of buckles, which are attached as follows. Try the belt and buckle on, marking the correct buckle position before sewing.

◇ *Clasp buckle* Slip the unfinished ends of the belt through the buckle. Turn the ends to the inside when the correct measurement mark is level with the bar of the buckle. Trim the ends to 2 in (5 cm). Turn in the raw ends and whipstitch to the belt.

◇ *Slide buckle* Finish off one end of the belt. Attach the other end of the belt to the buckle as for the clasp buckle. If the belt will be subject to stress, use snap fasteners to reinforce the buckle.

◇ *Prong buckle* Stitch a rectangle through all layers of fabric for the prong slit. Cut through this and insert the prong, folding the belt to the inside over the bar. Turn in the raw edge, and whipstitch to the belt. Finish the shaped end by making eyelets as for buttonholes, or using a commercial kit.

◇ *Half buckles* These are attached like prong buckles, but have a fabric loop to hold the belt end. Make the loop large enough for two thicknesses of belt. Position the buckle and sew the loop to the inside of the belt, before sewing down the end of the belt.

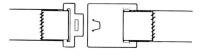

4.2 A clasp buckle fitted

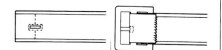

4.3 A prong buckle fitted

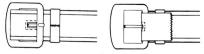

4.4 A half-buckle fitted

BUTTONS

Buttons are a way of fastening garments, and are also decorative accessories. Choose buttons wisely, with the following points in mind. Would the garment look best with a harmonizing colour, or a contrast? Textured buttons are interesting, but sometimes are not compatible for wear with a rough fabric. Plan how you will close the garment – with a loop, a buttonhole, a chain? Too big a button can overpower the dress; remember to think of size and proportion.

There are now many kinds of buttons you can cover yourself, with whatever fabric you choose. Be sure to have your button before making the buttonhole, as it is a much more difficult job to match a button to a buttonhole. Follow the pattern instructions for size and amount of buttons, as this has been clearly thought out by the designer and will be the most complementary to the garment. Use a strong, good-quality thread for sewing buttons on to the garment.

◆ SEW-THROUGH BUTTONS

A thread shank must be made whilst you are sewing the button in place to prevent the fabric around the closure from being distorted. The shank should be as long as the garment is thick at the buttonhole, plus 1/8 in (3 mm) for movement. Form the shank by putting a toothpick or cocktail stick over the button between the holes; sew over this when attaching the button. When the button is secure, remove the stick and wind the thread tightly under the button to form the shank; securely fasten the thread to the shank.

◆ SHANK BUTTONS

These are attached with small stitches sewn through the built-in shank. An additional thread shank may be needed for very thick fabric. If you would like your shank buttons to be detachable, insert metal shanks through the eyelets and fasten on with toggles.

◆ REINFORCED BUTTONS

These are necessary on coats, suits and delicate fabrics. For coats, place a small flat button on the inside of the garment directly under the outer button and sew from one to the other, making thread shanks as needed. On delicate fabrics substitute a small folded square of ribbon or seam binding. This should be placed between garment and facing at openings.

◆ JEWELLED AND FANCY BUTTONS

These often have very rough surfaces and can damage the garment. Sew the buttons directly to the buttonhole. Use snap fasteners behind the buttonhole to secure the opening.

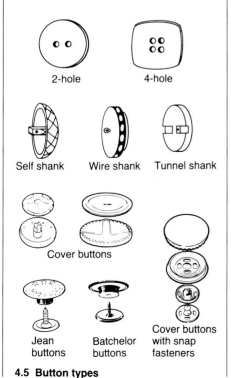

2-hole   **4-hole**

Self shank   **Wire shank**   **Tunnel shank**

Cover buttons

Jean buttons   **Batchelor buttons**   **Cover buttons with snap fasteners**

4.5 Button types

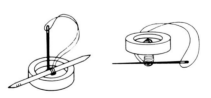

4.6 Sew-through buttons

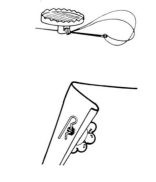

4.7 Shank buttons

4.8 Reinforced buttons

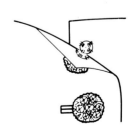

4.9 Jewelled buttons

HOOKS AND EYES

Hooks and eyes come in a variety of designs for special holding purposes. The standard type is made of brass, nickel or black-enamel-coated metal. Use nickel or brass hooks and eyes on light colours, and black ones on dark colours. Sizes start at 00, which is tiny, and progress to over an inch long. Covered hooks and eyes are made for use on coats, furs and similar items.

◆ LAPPED EDGES

On waistbands and other edges that lap, sew the hook slightly inside the overlap edge to conceal it. Fasten a straight eye in a corresponding position on the underlap. To attach, secure the thread and sew the hook on with oversew stitches worked around the circular holes. Pick up a garment thread with each stitch. Slip the needle under the fabric to the end of the hook and stitch to keep it flat; secure the thread.

◆ MEETING EDGES

Sew the hook to the garment as for lapped edges, positioning it 1/16 in (1.5 mm) inside one garment edge. Use a curved eye extending slightly beyond the other edge. Fasten with oversew stitches around the circular holes and small stitches to hold the sides of the eye flat to the garment.

◆ COVERED HOOKS AND EYES

For a really professional finish, cover the hooks and eyes with thread to match the garment. A better result is obtained if the hook and eye are sewn into place first and then covered completely with close blanket stitches.

Hook and eye tape

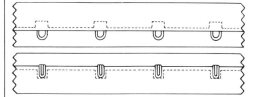

Hook and eyelette tape

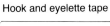

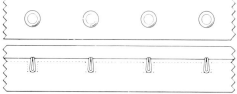

Hooks and loops   Hooks and eyes

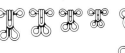 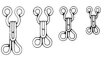

4.10 Hooks and eyes

Trouser or skirt hook and bar

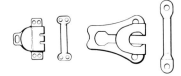

Waistband   Hooks and bars

Three position hook and eye

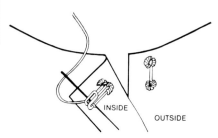

4.11 Hook and eye for lapped edge

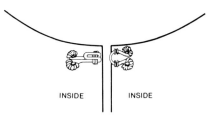

4.12 Hook and eye for a meeting edge

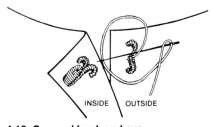

4.13 Covered hook and eye

SNAP FASTENERS

Snap fasteners are available in many sizes and types. Usually the fasteners are made of nickel, brass or black-enamel-coated metal. The size range is very extensive. Clear, see-through nylon snap fasteners are also available. Four-piece fasteners are strong enough to withstand hard wear and are ideal for children's clothes, sportswear and work clothes.

Snaps are one of the easiest closures to apply. Attach the ball section, which has a small protruding knob, to the overlapped garment. The socket section, which has a corresponding indentation, is applied to the underlapping garment. Snap fasteners will open under normal strain, and therefore use only in areas where there is little stress. Mark overlap where the fastener is to be placed, and put the ball section in this place. Sew to the garment with small close oversew stitches through each hole, picking up a garment thread with each

Snap fasteners are available through from size 000 to 10

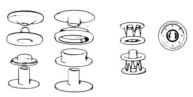

Four-piece press fasteners

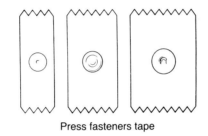

Press fasteners tape

4.14 Snap fasteners

stitch; secure the thread. To position the socket section, rub some tailor's chalk on the ball of the attached section of the fastener; close the edges of the garment, marking the correct place with the chalk. Sew in the same way as the ball section.

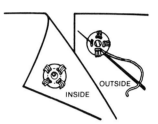

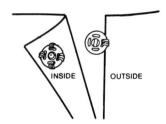

4.15 Fitting a snap fastener

TOUCH AND CLOSE FASTENER (VELCRO)

The touch and close fastener consists of a pile strip of tape and a hook strip of tape that interlock when the two are pressed together. It is sold by the yard or metre, and can be attached in strips or shapes to fit a closure area. It is easy to use, and ideal in many dressmaking and home sewing applications.

For flexibility the pile strip with the soft fluffy loops is applied to the overlap and the strip of tiny nylon hooks to the underlap. Both strips may be either hand or machine sewn to the garment.

This type of fastener can also be obtained in button-sized spots and applied by the same methods.

4.16 Touch and close fastener

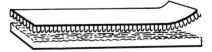

A touch – and it's closed

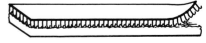

Just peel – and it's open

ZIPPERS

A zip is a strong and secure way to fasten a garment. It is also used in household sewing for closures on cushions and covers, and of course with accessories such as bags and holdalls.

Zippers can be concealed in a seamline, or can be used as a fashion feature in which the teeth are blatantly obvious. Colour can discreetly match or be a brilliant contrast. Zip insertion is covered in Part 5.

Zips are available from 10 cm (4 in) to 75 cm (30 in) in length. It is false economy to choose too short a zip: strain on the opening will cause the zip to break. A hook and eye at the top opening will also take strain away from the zip slider and teeth. The actual opening will be 13 mm (1/2 in) shorter than the zip size.

Fitted garments require longer zips than loose garments. Keep the zip closed at all times when measuring and fitting. Never cut away any zip tape: it supports the teeth. Sew the zip seam and put in the zip before the other seams are joined and before facings and waistbands are attached, except for invisible zippers which are sewn into place *before* the seam is joined.

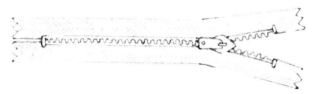

4.17 Zip

◆ ZIP TYPES AVAILABLE

◇ *Polyester* For man-made and lightweight fabrics – dresses, skirts and trousers. Machine washable, drip dry, shrink resistant. Closed at one end.

◇ *Nylon* As for polyester. Mainly for lightweight man-made fibres.

◇ *Metal dress and skirt* Lightweight, with coloured metal teeth on cotton tape. Closed at one end.

◇ *Invisible* To give a concealed finish to the opening: teeth are turned inwards by the runner. Also good for fine fabrics to avoid the teeth catching.

◇ *Open ended* For jackets, cardigans, body warmers. Medium-weight zips with metal or nylon teeth.

◇ *Extra strong* For trousers or jeans. Metal teeth.

◇ *Fashion chunky* In metal, or more often bright coloured nylon.

WAISTBAND STIFFENERS

◆ CURVED PETERSHAM

This can be used instead of a waistband. Usually available in 25 mm widths and curved to make it more comfortable in wear. The colours are limited to black and white. Nylon petersham is fast to washing, as is the curve, and also shrink resis-tant. Rayon petersham may have to be dry-cleaned.

◆ STRAIGHT PETERSHAM

Straight petersham is excellent for using inside a waistband. There are usually more widths and colours available than for curved petersham, although 25 mm black and white are still the most popular. The polyester variety is colour fast and will not soften or shrink when washed. Rayon petersham may have to be dry-cleaned.

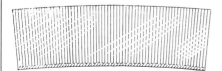

4.18 Curved petersham

4.19 Straight petersham

FOLD-A-BAND

◆ VILENE

Vilene Firm Fold-a-Band is produced with three rows of slots, gives an accurate guide for quick and easy folding and sewing.

The outer slots help to attach the waistband to the garment in a perfectly straight sewing line. The centre row of slots give an exact guide line for folding the top edge of the Waistband straight simply iron on, stitch, fold and stitch.

For fast easy accurate waistbands, place Fold-a-Band on to the waist-

4.20

band, cover with a damp cloth and press with a warm dry iron.

Fold-a-Band is a permanent way to hold pleats and folds in one easy application. The Fold-a-Band, with a single row of slots, reinforces lighter-weight fabrics. At the same time the slots give a sharply defined line to all straight edges. It is ideal for all small applications. Simply iron on fold and press. For cuffs, pleats, pockets and plackets, place Fold-a-Band on to the fabric, cover with a damp cloth, then press with a warm dry iron.

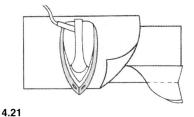

4.21

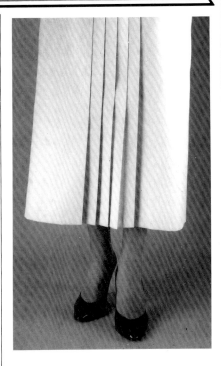

4.22 Pleated skirts using Vilene Fold-a-Band

TRIMMINGS

◆ BRAID

Braid is available in a variety of widths, in plain, woven or textured finishes, and in wool, cotton or man-made fibre. Choose from the following groups:

◇ *Braid* Flat; woven edge.
◇ *Soutache braid* Narrow bias woven braid, used to outline a rounded shape.
◇ *Flat embroidered braid*.
◇ *Ricrac braid* Woven-edge zigzag braid. Stitch down the centre or place behind a folded edge so that only the points show.
◇ *Folded braid* (military braid) Bias woven for enclosing raw edges. Plain, unpatterned. Ideal for binding jacket edges Chanel style.

4.23 Trimmings (McCabe)

◇ *Fringed braid* Predominantly used in soft furnishings; some dress weights.
◇ *Piped braid* Narrow piping cord woven inside plain coloured braid. (often called insertion piping.)

◆ RIBBON

Ribbon is available in a multitude of colours, widths and fibres to suit every possible need:

◇ *Plain ribbon* Flat, woven edge.
◇ *Fused edge ribbon* Mainly man-made fibres.
◇ *Printed patterned ribbon*
◇ *Velvet pile ribbon* Woven-edge cotton or fused man-made fibre.
◇ *Picot edge ribbon* Decorative knotted edges.

THREADS

Threads are most important: for good results, always use good thread. There is a wide selection of cotton, polyester and polycotton threads in an enormous range of colours. For dressmaking and other general sewing projects it is important to use the correct thread for the type of fabric you are stitching, and to have the *same* thread on the bobbin and on the top of the machine. For embroidery and decorative stitching (including top stitching) the choice of threads will enhance the design not only with colour but also with texture. From very fine embroidery silks and cottons through to extremely heavy bold and buttonhole twists, the choice is tremendous.

When experimenting with the sewing machine it is a good idea to try the stitches out with various

4.24

threads to gauge the different effects. However, it should be remembered that modern precision machines cannot always cope if a very thick thread is put on the bobbin *as well as* through the needle; there is just not enough room in the raceway. It is advisable to leave a normal sewing thread on the bobbin when using thick buttonhole threads on the top. If there are a number of colours on a design it is a good idea to use a bobbin thread that matches the fabric colour; this saves changing the bobbin every time you change the top thread colour.

When trying out stitches and various threads, note the fine adjustments available for stitch length in particular. To get a denser satin stitch you need to reduce the stitch length nearly to 0. With a very fine polyester thread the setting will be much lower than with, say, a buttonhole twist. You will also find that satin stitch patterns look much heavier and more important with a heavy thread, and the open-work patterns (stretch embroidery stitches) much more spidery and delicate with the very fine threads. In craft, embroidery and decorative work the combination of stitches and threads can become an art form in its own right.

For general sewing, follow the easy guidelines on the accompanying chart. In addition, note the following:

◇ *Pure fabrics/fibres* (cotton, silk, wool) can be sewn with 100 per cent cotton. On silk and wool try 100 per cent silk thread for a pleasant sewing experience and a professional finish. Pure fabrics can also be sewn with all-purpose thread – but they do vary in thickness, so choose carefully for the fabric you are using.

◇ *Nylons, polyester and other manmade fabrics* Must be stitched with a synthetic thread, and there are many to choose from. It is most important to have a certain amount of s-t-r-e-t-c-h in the thread to match that of the fabric. Also use these polyester threads on jerseys, stretch towelling, plush and knits so that the seams will not break when you stretch or bend.

◇ *Combination fabrics* Such as wool/polyester and polycotton can be sewn with most threads. However, if there is more than a small percentage of polyester, favour a polyester or a combination thread. Sylko Supreme is a mercerized cotton thread wrapped around a polyester core, and is ideal for these combination fabrics.

NEEDLES

◆ MACHINE NEEDLES

All machines come with a selection of needles, and manufacturers usually recommend that you use needles supplied by them for best results. It is true to say, however, that needle sizes are standard and thus normally interchangeable. This is particularly helpful with specialist needles such as wing and leather.

The most common fault when you have a new machine is to insert the needle wrongly. Manufacturers' handbooks clearly show this operation. I cannot overemphasize how important it is to put the needle in the correct way around: you just cannot stitch at all if it is not inserted correctly.

It is most important to replace your needles regularly. Needles go

blunt surprisingly quickly, especially when you are using synthetic fabrics. It is a good habit to change the needle after making every garment or project. Remember to *throw it away*; do not retain it for reuse at a later date. Ballpoint needles are not *blunt* needles, and need to be changed regularly too. Blunt needles will damage fibres in your fabric and they will also start to skip stitches.

◆ CHOOSING THREAD ◆

Fabrics		Type	Threads	Continental machine needle	British machine needle
Fine fabrics Net, organdie, lace, lawn, voile, chiffon, tulle, silk		Natural	Sylko or Sylko Supreme	60–70	9–11
		Man-made	Gütterman or Sylko Supreme	60–70	9–11
Lightweight fabrics Gingham, muslin, fine poplin, taffeta, silk, seersucker, crêpe de Chine, wool challis, faille		Natural	Sylko or Sylko Supreme	70–90 scarfed	11–14
		Man-made and mixtures	Sylko Supreme or Gütterman	70–90 scarfed	11–14
Medium-weight fabrics Poplin, cotton, suitings, corduroy, linen, satin, brocade, velvet, raw silks, wool crêpe, bouclé		Natural	Sylko or Sylko Supreme	70–90 scarfed	11–14
		Man-made and mixtures	Gütterman or Sylko Supreme	70–90 scarfed	11–14
Heavyweight fabrics Tweed, gabardine, flannel, sailcloth, twill, denim, canvas, furnishings		Natural	Sylko or Sylko Supreme	90–110	14–18
		Man-made and mixtures	Sylko Supreme	90–110	14–18
Stretch fabrics Silk and cotton jersey, polyester jersey, single and double knits, plush, stretch towelling *Use stretch stitch wherever possible*	Lightweight	Natural	Sylko plus stretch stitch, otherwise Sylko Supreme	60–70 ball or scarfed	9–11 ball or scarfed
		Man-made and mixtures	Sylko Supreme or Gütterman	60–70 ball or scarfed	9–11 ball or scarfed
	Heavyweight	Natural	Sylko plus stretch stitch, otherwise Sylko Supreme	70–90 ball or scarfed	11–14 ball or scarfed
		Man-made and mixtures	Sylko Supreme or Gütterman	70–90 ball or scarfed	11–14 ball or scarfed
Special fabrics	PVC	Man-made	Sylko Supreme	90–100	14–16
	Suede/leather and imitation	Natural	Sylko or strong thread	Spear or 90–110	14–18
		Man-made	Sylko Supreme	Leather point	
	Also: Pure silks and pure medium and heavyweight wools	Natural	Kirkame pure silk thread	70–90	11–14
Top stitching Lightweight fabrics		All types	Sylko or Sylko Supreme	60–90 carfed or ball if appropriate	9–14 scarfed or ball if appropriate
Medium-weight fabrics		All types	Sylko or Sylko Supreme: two threads	90–110	14–18
Heavyweight fabrics		All types	Bold or Gütterman button twist	90–110	14–18

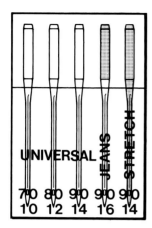

UNIVERSAL   JEANS   STRETCH

70   80   90   90   90
10   12   14   16   14

4.25

Stitches may also skip if your needle is too small or too large for the fabric you are stitching: for example, an 18 on crêpe de Chine or an 11 on denim. You may also find the same problem occurring if you use an extremely fine thread with an 18 needle: the hook just does not make the stitch.

The following are various needle types:

◇ *Scarfed, ballpoint and perfect stitch* needles are designed to cope with synthetics and jersey fabric. However, they sew beautifully on pure fabrics too: knits or wovens (cotton, silk, wool), and mixtures such as polycotton and wool/silk.

◇ *Teflon* needles are for heavier synthetics, jersey, double knits, and Crimplene or bulked fibres, plushes, single knits, knits and PVC.

◇ *Jeans* needles slice through denim with ease. Use also on heavier upholstery work, tents, canvas sails and similar tasks.

◇ *Leather* needles have a blade rather than a normal point; this will slice through leather without damaging the skins. Use normal settings on your machine, and a cotton or all-purpose thread for stitching seams. Embroidery on leather is perfectly practicable; in this instance the buttonhole twist can give excellent results (finer thread on the bobbin), but Sylko and even the pure silk threads look marvellous too.

◇ *Twin* needles are very neglected and can be both practical and decorative (see Part 5).

◇ *Triple* needles can be used on a limited number of machines and are used similarly to twin needles. Check your handbook before using.

◇ *Wing* needles are designed especially for hem-stitched decorative finishes and are very simple to use. A good range of hem stitches is available on some machines, but utility stitches (even straight and zigzag) can be sewn with the needle for interesting effects. A twin-wing needle is a progression from the wing needle, and the comments on both twin and wing needles apply.

◆ HAND SEWING NEEDLES

To complement machine stitching, you need to sew by hand. Experts sew quicker with a short needle, so try the betweens needles – the tailor's needle – which is shorter than sharps and easier to ply. You also need an assortment of heavy-duty household and craft needles.

The following list gives the main needle types:

◇ *Sharps* Medium length, oval-eyed, all-purpose needles for plain hand sewing.

◇ *Betweens* Same as sharps but shorter. For fine detailed hand work; can be used for quilting. Also called tailor's needles.

◇ *Crewel* For hand embroidery. Same as sharps but with extra long eye for embroidery threads.

◇ *Darner* For mending. Long needle to reach across holes and weave around edges with long eye to take thick thread. May also be used for basting.

◇ *Long darner* Same as darner but longer. For mending thick fabrics.

◇ *Tapestry* Short, thick-eyed, blunt-point needle for canvas embroidery.

◇ *Ballpoint or unipoint* A rounded-point hand or machine needle for sewing knitted fabrics. Point pushes between yarns and does not pierce them, so preventing fabric from unravelling.

◇ *Millinery* Long thin hand sewing needle with small round eye for millinery, long basting stitches. Can be used for quilting.

◇ *Beading* Straight fine hand sewing needle with long eye for threading beads, pearls and so on.

◇ *Upholstery* Large curved needle for sewing upholstery or furniture.

◇ *Bodkin* Thick needle with blunt end, long eye. For threading cords, ribbons, tapes.

INTERFACING, UNDERLINING AND LINING

There can be confusion between interfacing, underlining and lining. Interfacing and underlining are classed as haberdashery, whilst lining is generally found with the fabrics.

◆ UNDERLINING

Underlining is normally used on a sheer, fine or unstable fashion fabric. It is cut on the same lines as the top fabric; the two are then pinned and basted (tacked) together and made up as one. It is important to achieve the desired effect and drape of the fashion fabric; the interlining must therefore be chosen with care, and must have the same drapability and handle as the other fabric.

◆ LINING

Lining differs from underlining and interfacing in that it lines the inside of a garment to finish it off neatly, and it keeps the item of clothing from stretching out of shape: it does not mould the silhouette, but merely preserves it. Lining should be smooth and feel nice against the skin, and it should be lighter in weight than the fashion fabric so that it does not distort the shape of the garment.

◆ INTERFACING

Interfacing comes in two types – woven and non-woven. It can also be either sew-in or iron-on (fusible). The interfacing helps to mould the garment and support the fabric, and often different types and weights can be used in a single outfit.

Woven interfacing must be cut following the grain lines marked on the pattern pieces.

Wovens are made from a variety of fabrics:

◇ *Buckram* Woven cotton which is very stiff and hard. Suitable for a wide range of handicraft and furnishing uses. Do not wash or dry clean.

◇ *Collar canvas* Pure flax, stiff and medium weight, for use in collars in jackets and coats. Dry clean.

◇ *Hollands* Pure flax cloth which is firm but not stiff. This fabric is often referred to as 'shrunk duck'. Use in tailoring for facings in men's and women's jackets and coats. Hollands should be well dampened and ironed before final cutting to avoid further shrinkage. Dry clean.

◇ *Haircloth* Similar to hollands but somewhat thicker and stiffer, and so more suitable for heavier and thicker coats and jackets. Preshrink before final cutting. Dry clean.

◇ *Lawn* Fine cotton weave used to interface collars, cuffs and fronts of blouses and dresses. Washable. Buy shrunk, or preshrink before use.

◇ *Mull* Fine cotton interfacing used as lawn in thin dresses and blouses. Washable. Buy shrunk, or preshrink before use.

◇ *Permastiff* A firm cotton non-fusible interlining for use in collars and cuffs etc. for crisp, lightweight jackets and coats. Also suitable for some furnishing uses. Dry clean or wash.

◇ *Tropical* A lightweight version of haircloth in mixed fibres. Treat as haircloth. Dry clean.

Non-woven interfacing is made by fibres being fused together, and there is no straight of grain. Stretchable non-wovens must, however, follow the straight of grain so that the stretch is in the right direction.

The most often used non-woven is Vilene – a trade name that has become a generic term.

Make sure you choose an interfacing with the same washing and dry cleaning instruction as your chosen fabric. All Vilene interfacings are dry cleanable, except soft and firm iron-on. These become dry cleanable if kept in position by sewing and repressing.

Vilene types

◇ *Sew-in interfacings* Still preferred by some home dressmakers, these are often selected for fabrics such as velvet corduroy and seersucker. Sew-in qualities are available in light, medium and heavy weights.

◇ *Medium and firm iron-on interfacings* These give a crisp clean handle on wash-only fabrics. Improved over many years, Vilene medium and firm iron-on qualities are designed for use with 100 per cent cottons and cotton/synthetic blends – especially in small detail areas which need a clean crisp finish, particularly collars and cuffs.

◇ *Superstretch* The only interfacing designed for knitted fabrics. The difference an interfacing makes to knitted and jersey fabrics is evident in the appearance and wearability of a garment. But for an interfacing to succeed with these types of fabric it is important to match the stretch characteristics of knitteds. Superstretch is constructed to provide optimum stretch and shape retention and therefore to match the characteristics of knitted fabrics.

◇ *Pelmet, waistband and craft interfacings* These are extra heavy sew-in-qualities. Available in two widths, this type is recommended for use in craft work, handbags, belts, pelmets and waistbands, where a heavier firmer handle is required. It is also ideal for fabric painting, printing and collage work.

Hints and tips on Vilene use

1 Be guided by suggestions made on pattern instructions on where to use interfacings, but add others if necessary.

◆ VILENE INTERFACINGS ◆

Fabric weight	Suggested fabric	Recommended Vilene interfacing	Description	Application
Ultrasoft delicate	Voile, chiffon, silk, crêpe de Chine, lawn, georgette, polyester, cotton, polycotton, lightweight wools	Ultrasoft light 308 fusible white 309 fusible charcoal	No grainline non-stretch, soft to touch – yet stable control Washable and dry cleanable	Collars, cuffs, soft features, bows, yokes, full fronts, back yokes
Soft, delicate or lightweight	Polyester, silk, lawn, cotton, seersucker, panne velvet	Light sew-in 310 white 311 charcoal	No grainline Washable and dry cleanable	Collars, cuffs, facings, yokes
Light to medium	Challis, poplin, wool, wool blends, linen, cotton	Ultrasoft medium 315 fusible white	No grainline, non-stretch, soft to touch yet stable control Washable and dry cleanable	Collars, full fronts, back yokes for suits, sleeve edges, soft belts
Light to medium	Corduroy, velvet	Medium sew-in 312 white	No grainline washable and dry cleanable	
Medium to heavy	Gabardine, tweeds, suit and coat weight wools and woollen mixtures	Ultrasoft medium 316 white Ultrasoft heavy 316 white	No grainline, non-stretch, soft to touch yet stable Washable and dry cleanable	Full fronts, lapels, collars, shoulders, suits and coats, belts, craft applications
Medium to heavy		Heavy sew-in 313 white	No grainline Washable and dry cleanable	
Light to medium	Lightweight knits, jersey, polyester, double knits	Superstretch 319 white	Has grainline – lengthwise stability and crosswise stretch Washable and dry cleanable	Collars, cuffs, facings, soft features, bows, yokes, full fronts, sleeve edges
Light to medium	Cotton and cotton blend fabrics	Medium iron-on 304 white	No grainline, light crisp handle Washable only	Collars, cuffs, facings and other small-area applications
Medium to heavy	Cotton and cotton blend fabrics	Firm iron-on 305 white	No grainline, firm crisp handle Washable only	Collars, cuffs, facings and other small-area applications

2 Cut and fuse all your interfacing pieces in one stage to save time.

3 Ensure sew-ins lie completely flat on fabric before basting and sewing.

4 Choose charcoal interfacing on dark, sheer fabrics.

5 When interfacing plain, sheer fabrics, use a double layer of sheer fabric to prevent interfacing showing through.

6 Interface fabric edges that fray badly with strips of Vilene to make handling easier.

7 Save all left-over pieces of Vilene for small-area application.

8 Interfaced edges help eliminate puckered stitching, such as in zip areas, sleeve edges, top stitching and pockets.

9 Select sew-in qualities when using fabrics that require special handling such as pile fabrics, metallics, proofed and finished fabrics.

Preparation for applying interfacing

Whichever type of interfacing has been chosen, the preparation is the same. Once the pattern pieces have been cut out in the fabric, select those that require interfacing. Cut the interfacing to the same size as the fabric pieces.

Down the front opening of a blouse or shirt, it is often better to interface the facing rather than the wrong side of the main garment. Remember that a garment that is well made should invariably be interfaced in certain areas, but the interfacing should never be evident on the right side of the garment.

Whether interfacing should be applied to the top or under collar of a garment is dependent on the type of fabric and the type of interfacing. For example, it is often better to apply an iron-on interfacing to the top collar, as this gives a smoother finish and no bulk shows on the seams.

Method of application

◇ *Iron-on interfacings* Place iron-on interfacings in position with adhesive side face down on the wrong side of your fabric. Using a hot, dry iron, apply with a firm pressing action, *not* a sliding movement. Always test on a small piece of your fabric first to make sure the interfacing gives the right handle to your fabric. It is necessary to use a damp cloth with the hot, dry iron in order to achieve an effective bond. Always press until moisture has evaporated. Repress lightweight fabrics after washing.

◇ *Sew-in interfacings* These must be attached to the garment, either by inclusion into the seams (lightweight fabrics) or by catch stitching round the edges after trimming off the seam allowances (heavy fabrics). Place the interfacing piece to garment piece on wrong side and slip baste into position (remember to remove slip basting stitches at end). Catch stitch using small, invisible stitches along any folds. (This is not necessary if the fold is to be top or edge stitched afterwards.) Make up the garment in the usual way when the interfacing has been attached.

◆ VILENE SPEED TAILORING

The ready-to-wear clothing industry has used fusible interfacings for a considerable time. This method is now available for home dressmaking, and proficient use and making up will provide a professional and well-finished outfit.

◆ VILENE SPEED TAILORING GUIDE ◆

Speed tailoring
- The fastest method of making a jacket using Vilene fusible interfacings
- Uses up-to-date construction methods and products which cut sewing time in half
- Is a combination of techniques used by the clothing manufacturers to shape a garment professionally.
- Uses specially produced 100% Vilene shaped shoulder pads and sleeve heads to give couture finish to all jackets and coats.

Time saving tailoring tips

1 Select a style which is best for you. For speed, avoid patterns with time consuming details such as flap or welt pockets, back or sleeve vents.

2 Select a fabric which is easy for you to work with, i.e. wool, tweeds or linen types. Fabrics with a combination of synthetic and natural fibres are easiest to work with. Avoid fabrics which require special handling and extra care, such as plaids or napped fabrics. Preshrink your fabric.

3 Select your interfacing(s), always test on a small piece of fabric for desired handle and drapability. New ulstrasoft easy fuse iron-on interfacings are recommended from the Vilene range for speed tailoring. A combination of interfacings may be used, to give extra stability in area that may need this, i.e. under collar. Recommendations are give below.

| Ultrasoft light | | No. 308 | White | Lend gentle, smooth control to upper collar, lapel |
| Ultrasoft light | | No. 309 | Charcoal | and facing, jacket front and back. |

| Ultrasoft medium | | No. 315 | White | Adds control to under collar. |

| Ultrasoft heavy | ⁴⁄₅₀ | No. 316 | White ℗ | Subtle shaping for heavier tailored fabrics. |

However, fabric is the most important consideration when choosing an interfacing and fabric – guidelines are given below:

Ultrasoft light No. 308/No. 309	Ultrasoft medium No. 315	Ultrasoft heavy No. 316
Lightweight fabrics such as polyester, silk, voile, georgette, crêpe de Chine, cotton, polycottons, lawn. Lightweight wools etc.	Medium weight wool. blends and tweeds. Wool gaberdine, crêpe, wool flannel, wool jersey, medium weight viscose, linen and linen looks.	Heavier tweeds, worsteds wools, wool blends and coatings.

4 Cut out fabric following layout on pattern guide sheet and then cut out interfacing. We recommend that interfacings include seam allowances, to ensure a clean sharp line at seam edges, but may be slightly trimmed down when a heavy interfacing is used.

5 Fuse correctly 'the key to a perfect bond'
Use a damp cloth.
Use a warm dry iron.
Press iron firmly in place, at least
15 seconds per section
(do not slide iron)

(continued overleaf)

VILENE SPEED TAILORING GUIDE (cont.)

Time saving tailoring techniques

Under collar

Using pattern piece, cut interfacing.
Fuse interfacing to both halves of under collar.
Stitch centre back seam and trim, press flat.

Upper collar

The upper collar and front facing are joined
by the same seam, therefore use the same
quality of interfacing. This will give a smooth
continuous line from the collar to the lapel.
Using pattern piece, cut interfacing.

Front facing

Using front facing pattern
pieces cut interfacing.

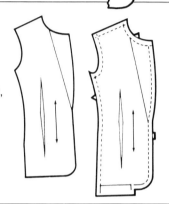

Jacket front

Important – decide how much support is necessary for your fabric and style.

Method 1	Method 2
Use jacket fronts shaped interfacing pattern piece. Pink the outer edges of interfacing if your fabric is lightweight to avoid a ridge.	Use entire front jacket pattern piece to cut interfacing. (If desired when using heavy Ultrasoft, trim Interfacing from dart areas and seam allowances to reduce bulk before fusing.)

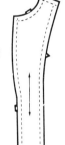

Back interfacing

Trim down back interfacing pattern piece so it measures approximately 7.5 cm (3 in) in length. This allows for
greater mobility when using fusible interfacings.
Select the same interfacing as for the jacket front. Pink the outer edges of the interfacing if your fabric is lightweight
to avoid a ridge. Sew jacket sections together.

Jacket hems or pocket edges

Trim one side of light fold-a-band leaving approximately 1cm (³⁄₈ in).
Position slotted rows of light fold-a-band over jacket hem or pocket fold.
Trim 1.3 cm (½ in) from seam allowances to reduce bulk. Fuse.
Fold on slotted line and press. Also use light fold-a-band on vents and
sleeve hems. To 'tack' hem into place, fuse a small square of
Wundaweb between seam allowance and hem.

Shaped shoulder pads – 100% Vilene

Smooth and contour the whole shoulder area, they fill out a hollow just below the shoulder.
Available in three sizes and two raglan sizes.

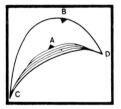
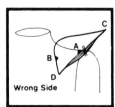
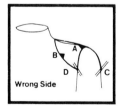
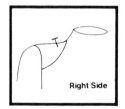

Notch extends ¼ in into the sleeve at shoulder seam. B-notch to front C and D. Along sleeve seam allowance.	Tack pad at Point A to sleeve seam allowance.	Tack pad at Points C and D and turn to RS.	Check for fit and pin outer curved edge to neck edge on shoulder seam line. Tune to WS and stitch at this point. Stitch along sleeve seam allowance between C and D.

VILENE SPEED TAILORING GUIDE (cont.)

Shaped sleeve head – 100% Vilene
Are placed around the top of the sleeve to create a smooth line and support the roll at the sleeve cap preventing 'caved in' sleeves.
Line notch up with shoulder point on armhole edge. Stitch sleeve head along 1.5 cm (⅝ in) seam allowance. Turn sleeve head into sleeve cap.

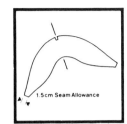

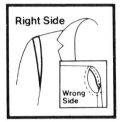

Lining
Machine stitch the lining pieces following the pattern instructions.
Sew your jacket upper collar and front facing together and stitch them to your lining shell.
With right sides together, stitch the lining and facings to the jacket, matching notches and dots.
Grade and clip the seams. Turn it right side out and press. Hem the lining by slipstitching into place.
Remember – give the lining room to 'move'.

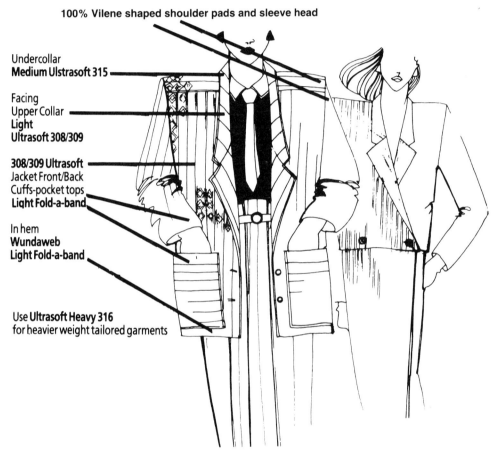

100% Vilene shaped shoulder pads and sleeve head

Undercollar
Medium Ulstrasoft 315

Facing
Upper Collar
**Light
Ultrasoft 308/309**

308/309 Ultrasoft
Jacket Front/Back
Cuffs-pocket tops
Light Fold-a-band

In hem
**Wundaweb
Light Fold-a-band**

Use **Ultrasoft Heavy 316**
for heavier weight tailored garments

These recommendations are given as a general guideline only. Always select your Vilene interfacings to suit fabric and style.

5 · STITCHES AND TECHNIQUES

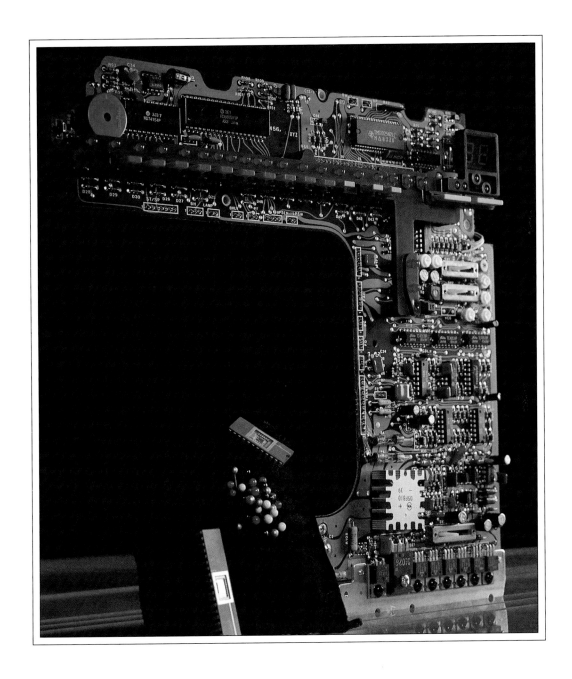

STITCHES

The term *stitch* is used widely to denote various end results. Thus a label 'stitch' can denote anything from a series of stitches in a straight line to a number of stitches in quite complicated stitch formation with a general term, e.g. feather stitch. To complicate matters, some machine companies may call the same stitch formation a *pattern* – and having called it a pattern they may then call it by a completely different name (this happens particularly in multilanguage books). It is not necessarily named wrongly; descriptions just do differ. For example, 'overlock' is a patented name despite the fact that it is used so often to describe various stitches that perform this particular function; overcast, overedge and so on are therefore often substituted.

There are also stitch terms crossing those of techniques; 'blind hem' is a stitch sequence, but it is also a technique with a specialist presser foot.

To try and bring some order to a description of stitching, in this section are listed machine stitches (stitch patterns or stitch sequences) and their most common names, with alternative names where known. (At least most companies tend to use the same symbols to denote the stitches.) In the next section will be listed techniques, and the same names may be used again if necessary (as with the example just given of 'blind hem').

◆ UTILITY STITCHES

Straight stitch

A straight stitch can be sewn at the left, centre or right of the presser foot, and often with even more variations of position. Use it to hold two or more fabrics together, as in seams, darts, tucks, pin tucks, top stitching, narrow hem, rolled hem, quilting, gathering, edge stitching and patchwork. (See also twin needle sewing.)

Straight stretch stitch

(reinforced stretch stitch, triple stretch stitch, triple strength stitch)

Use this as straight stitch on a fabric with stretch properties – stable knits, double knits, machine knitwear, stretch terry, plush, velour, sweatshirt and sportswear fabrics, and Crimplene. Do *not* use this stitch on very fine, silky jersey as it is too heavy and will pucker the fabric.

Because this stitch sequence includes a backstitch it is also very strong. Use when strength is required on denim, canvas, upholstery, trouser zips, crotch seams, armholes, bags and holdalls.

If there is no specially formulated saddle stitch on the machine, this stitch can substitute as a top stitch to good effect. Use it with one or two sewing threads (thread two

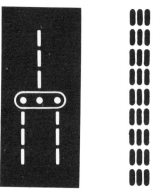

5.1 Straight stitch   **5.2 Straight stretch stitch**

5.3 Zigzag stitch   **5.4 Outline zigzag stitch**

strands as one through the top threading system and use one needle), or a bold buttonhole twist (here leave the normal sewing thread on the bobbin).

Zigzag

The basic zigzag stitch can be adapted by the user for many tasks. It is the accepted and original overedge, neatening stitch; it has been superseded by many better alternatives, but is still useful for this function on occasions. As with all patterns which incorporate stitch width, the actual width is crucial. Do make it *narrower* if any sort of puckering or bad stitch formation occurs.

Zigzag can be used in a multitude of width and length permutations on all fabrics to overedge, appliqué and stitch over cords and braids (couching), to apply shirring and other fine elastics, to appliqué and attach lace, and with the twin needle.

When the stitch is adjusted to a very low number on the stitch length so that the stitches lie closely side by side, this is called *satin stitch*. This can be obtained manually on override after programming the basic zigzag stitch. Satin stitch is used widely for appliqué of all kinds.

Outline zigzag

Careful scrutiny will show this to be different from standard zigzag. Instead of diagonal stitch penetration, here two small stitches are taken side by side. The machine then moves forward to the next pair of stitches, and so on. The zigzag thus created is Z shaped. This is a very narrow stitch (usually setting 1 wide) and is used on bulked fabrics where that width will be lost in the bulk of the fibres. It is an alternative to straight stretch stitch on stretch towelling, Crimplene and knitwear. It is a very stretchy stitch.

Tricot zigzag

(multiple zigzag, multistitch zigzag, three-step zigzag, elastic stitch)

Designed as a stretch zigzag, this stitch can replace basic zigzag on many occasions. It is much better to overcast an edge with this stitch as it is firmer and flatter and holds more fibres in place. Use it, too, where you want strength and/or stretch.

Apply elastic with this zigzag on lingerie or children's wear for elasticated cuffs, ankles and waistlines.

Various darn sequences are available on computer machines. This stitch is an alternative: run backwards and forwards over the damaged or slit area for an extremely firm and efficient darn. It is advisable to place a small piece of interfacing or lining fabric behind the darn to give added strength if the fabric has worn thin.

Ricrac

(stretch triple zigzag)

This stitch is designed to sew high-stretch fabrics such as Lycra for swimwear and underwear, and to repair or join elastic. It is also an effective top stitch if used quite narrow.

Elastic casing

This is to sew over and make a casing for an elastic strip. Ensure that the side stitches are just *over* the elastic edges. The stitch is used for wrists and ankles on children's wear.

Blind hem

This stitch is used to turn up hems on garments and curtains. For the techniques, see the next section.

The stitch will also give a shell tuck or shell edging on fine fabrics; the top tension may need to be increased slightly.

Stretch blind hem

(zigzag blind stitch)

This is the hem stitch for stretch fabrics. Use it as for the previous stitch.

5.5 Tricot zigzag stitch

5.6 Ricrac stitch

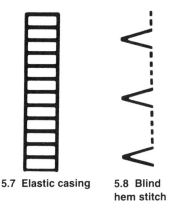

5.7 Elastic casing

5.8 Blind hem stitch

5.9 Zigzag blind stitch

5.10 Flatlock stitch

5.11 Knit stitch

5.12 Stretch overlock stitch

Flatlock

(closed overlock, stretch overlock)

This is designed to sew overlapped seams, decorative hems, binding or elastic on to woven and elastic/stretch fabrics.

The stitch is suitable as a seam and neatening process to give a double-stitched edge. Stitch on the seamline and trim away the excess seam allowance afterwards.

Knit stitch

(overlock, serge)

This is an all-in-one operation to provide a seam and neaten the edges, and is designed for knitted and stretch fabrics. It is, however, often suitable on various other cloths. (Serge is the American term for overlock.)

Stretch overlock

As the name implies, this provides a stretch seam and neatens in one operation.

Double-edge zigzag

This is an excellent seam and over-edge finish on fabrics that tend to fray more, such as linen and gabardine. Two zigzags are simultaneously worked over the fabric edge.

Overlock

(professional overlock)

This provides a seam, a zigzag over-edge and a chain or purl of threads off the edge between the zigzag stitches. It simulates various commercial overlock finishes.

5.13 Double-edge zigzag stitch

5.14 Overlock stitch

◆ CRAFT STITCHES

Feather stitch

This is an excellent copy of the hand embroidery stitch. Use it for patchwork and faggotting and other decorative work.

It is an extremely stretchy stitch, and so is ideal to use on elasticated lingerie items and swimwear.

Because the formation is basically that of the straight stretch stitch – but with zigzag width! – it is also very strong. Use it on domestic items, upholstery and luggage when a strong but more decorative than utilitarian finish is required.

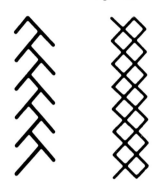

5.15 Feather stitch   **5.16 Smocking stitch**

Smocking stitch

This is a decorative stitch to give a smocked appearance. It is particularly useful on children's wear and lingerie.

Paris point

Paris point is a decorative hem stitch for household linens. It can look particularly effective when sewn with a wing needle.

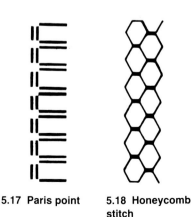

5.17 Paris point   **5.18 Honeycomb stitch**

Honeycomb

This is suitable for various finishes on lingerie and linings.

Scallop stitch

This forms a scallop shape made of straight running stitches. The width and length of the scallop can be adjusted by adjusting the stitch width and length control. It can be used for a hem in dress or for curtains and blinds. The three steps are stitch, trim and turn (Figure 5.20).

It can provide a scallop edge for frills and collars in dress and as a

5.19 Scallop stitch

Stitch length	Variations
5	
3.5	
2.5	

Variations of scallop stitch length using manual stitch length.

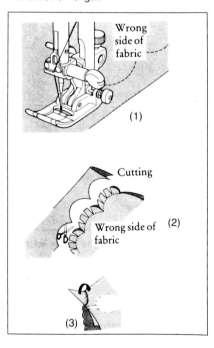

5.20 A turned scalloped hem.
Fold hem with right sides together. Sew scallops 10 mm (3/8 in) from folded edge (1). Trim close to stitching, leaving 3 mm (1/8 in) seam allowance. Clip seams as shown (2) or trim with pinking shears. Turn hem to right side and press (3).

finish for household linen, as follows. Sew around the edge of the item concerned; place the edge of the presser foot on the edge of the fabric. Then, using the stitching line as a guide, stitch over the top with a satin stitch. Trim the edges very close to the stitching afterwards with sharp scissors (Figure 5.21).

Note that the presser foot must be raised and the fabric repositioned at the end of each scallop. You must complete each scallop with the needle consistently on the left or the right because each will give a different effect to the finished work.

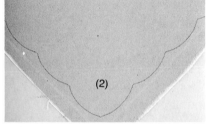
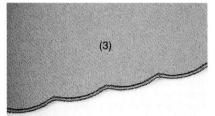
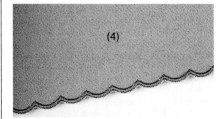

5.21 Decorative satin-stitched scallop edge using the straight stitch scallop as a guide (Bernina)

Saddle stitch

The exact stitch make-up or sequence of saddle stitches can vary in appearance, but they are designed to perform the same task – a pronounced top-stitch line for dress.

It can also provide an effective heavy straight line for various uses in crafts, including quilting.

Blanket stitch

Designed for appliqué work, this is more of a decorative finish than the basic zigzag stitch. It has the appearance of its hand-sewn equivalent.

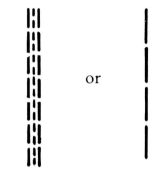

or

5.22 Saddle stitch

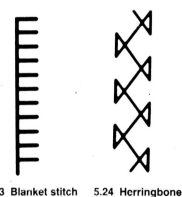

5.23 Blanket stitch   **5.24 Herringbone stitch**

5.25 Greek key stitch   **5.26 Vine stitch**

5.27 Machine embroidery (New Home)

Herringbone

Use this for faggotting and general decorative stitching.

Greek key

This stitch is also used for faggotting and general decorative stitching.

Vine stitch

This is basically a decorative stitch, but it is extremely stretchy and suitable for finishing hems on fine jersey fabrics. Some stitches are both decorative and utilitarian, which adds to their desirability and increases the scope of the machine.

Remember that *any* stitch sequence that combines backwards and forwards movement of the feed with the side to side needle movement will s-t-r-e-t-c-h. Even the pure embroidery stitches can be used on a variety of stretch fabrics.

The stitches illustrated for utility and craft work are those found on most makes of top machines. There are of course others which are only available on certain models.

◆ EMBROIDERY STITCHES

The variety of embroidery stitches is enormous, and I will not illustrate and name them all here! However, it is useful to note certain features of embroidery.

Satin stitch patterns

These are sometimes called block patterns or solid patterns. They are so called because to be sewn correctly they need a very close stitch length setting, that is satin stitch.

Openwork patterns

These are reverse stitch patterns, which are more lacy looking and include stitches such as feather and vine.

5.28 Satin stitch patterns

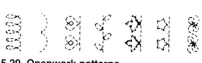

5.29 Openwork patterns

5.30 Scroll patterns

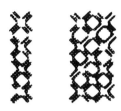

5.31 Cross-stitch patterns

Scroll patterns

These are extremely intricate embroidery sequences combining both some satin stitches and reverse stitches.

Cross-stitch

This is certainly embroidery; however, one cross-stitch is not particularly attractive by itself. Rows of stitches are aligned to form a design (Figure 5.32).

Hem stitching

There is quite a variety of these stitches. Again, a single unit is of little use by itself, but in a row or a combination of stitches it is a most successful adornment.

Free embroidery

This is the traditional form of free machine embroidery, in which the feed dog is dropped and the fabric is supported in a hoop which is moved freely under the needle by the operator to create the designs.

Pictogram

This is a computer machine technique. A series of preprogrammed stitch sequences can be chosen in any combination and programmed into memory by the operator to provide embroidered pictures or motifs.

Cartridge patterns

A cartridge system, combined with an embroidery unit, produces a range of motifs and monograms.

Free programming

Advanced computer sewing will enable stitch sequences to be put into memory to give the machinist complete freedom of design (Figure 5.36).

Alphabet sewing

The majority of computer machines perform alphabet and numerical stitching. Letters can be done in capitals, lower case and/or script depending on the make and model of machine (Figure 5.37).

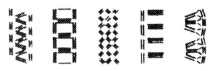

5.33 Hem stitching patterns

5.34 Pictogram patterns (Viking Husqvarna)

5.35 Cartridge patterns (Singer)

5.32 Cross-stitch embroidery (Viking)

5.36 Matching embroidery with china using free programming (Pfaff)

5.37 Alphabet sewing (New Home)

Stitch sequences

On a mechanical machine the stitches are selected and the length and width are manually set. Once obtained, the stitch will reproduce itself *ad infinitum*.

A computer machine is very different. When a stitch is selected, the machine will be automatically set for the desired stitch width and length. If the setting needs to be altered for any reason, this is done manually by override adjustments (Figure 5.38).

The ability to memorize stitch patterns and sequences gives great versatility to computer machines, allowing amazing scope in stitch mixing. The only way to discover the permutations of a machine is to experiment on it! The ability of computer machines to produce a mirror image also enhances the embroidery available. The variations can be very interesting, and basic or

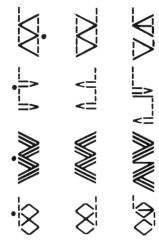

5.39 Basic stitches in mirror image

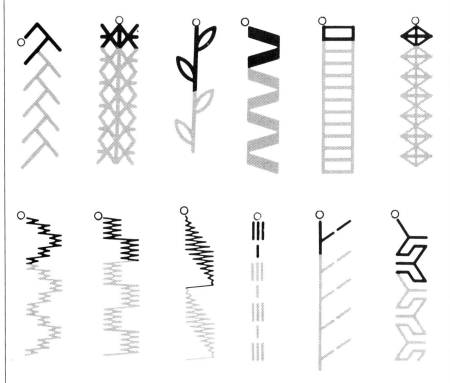

5.38 Stitch mixing. Illustrates the part of a continuous pattern selected when one memory is programmed.

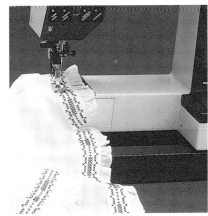

5.40 Mirror image embroidery (McCabe)

5.41 Constructing a motif using one pattern selection. Pattern 1 is programmed once. Each time the machine stops, the fabric is turned 90° clockwise to give motif 2. Turning anti-clockwise gives motif 3.

utility stitches mixed in with decorative or embroidery stitches produce surprising results (Figures 5.39 and 5.40). When you are experimenting, therefore, it is useful to mix anything and everything together to see what happens.

One-pattern selection

Some computer machines will allow you to program just one pattern; the machine will stop when that pattern is complete (Figure 5.41). Sometimes the machine will lock off automatically; sometimes you program it to stop and lock off. Programming one pattern at a time allows a motif to be constructed, or details to be inserted here and there into a design, or maybe just one arrowhead or bartack in dressmaking (Figure 5.42).

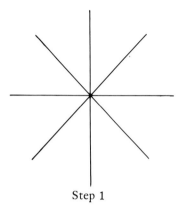

Step 1

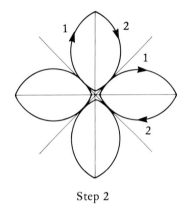

Step 2

Step 3

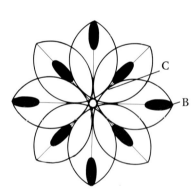

Step 4

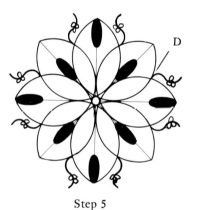

Step 5

5.42 Building up a motif using three stitches.
(1) Mark with chalk.
(2) Scallop stitch from centre to outside; turn, scallop back. Repeat.
(3) Performed similarly.
(4) Indicates points to start block pattern.
(5) Indicates point to start flower pattern and shows finished design.

TECHNIQUES

A *technique* is a specialist operation that you require the machine to perform, such as buttonholes, zipper insertion and quilting.

Techniques require a particular stitch to perform the operation, and they also usually require a specialist presser foot: when feet clip on and off easily, this is not a chore. If a specialist foot is provided it really is advisable to use it for best results. The recommended foot for the technique will be listed in the manufacturer's handbook, and in some cases can be indicated on the machine itself when the required stitch is programmed.

This section covers the main techniques available; they may be mentioned again in Part 6.

Presser feet

Presser feet come neatly stowed and labelled for easy reference. The illustrations show some examples of the presser feet provided by the various manufacturers.

5.43 Faggoting, pin tucking, shell edging, appliqué, patchwork, lace insertion, frills and gathers – all shown off to perfection! (McCabe)

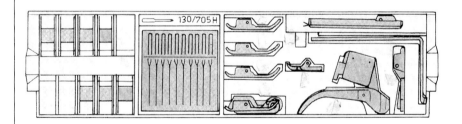

5.44 Presser feet, needles and bobbins stowed in the Pfaff *Creative*

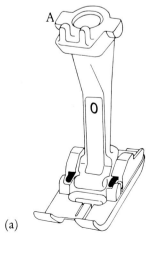

(a)

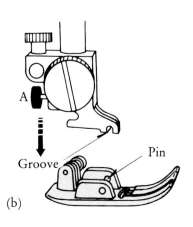

Groove   Pin

(b)

**5.45 (a) The Bernina presser foot and shank form a unit. This whole piece clips on to the presser bar at point A.
(b) Some clip-on feet also have a retaining spring. Button A is pushed to release foot.**

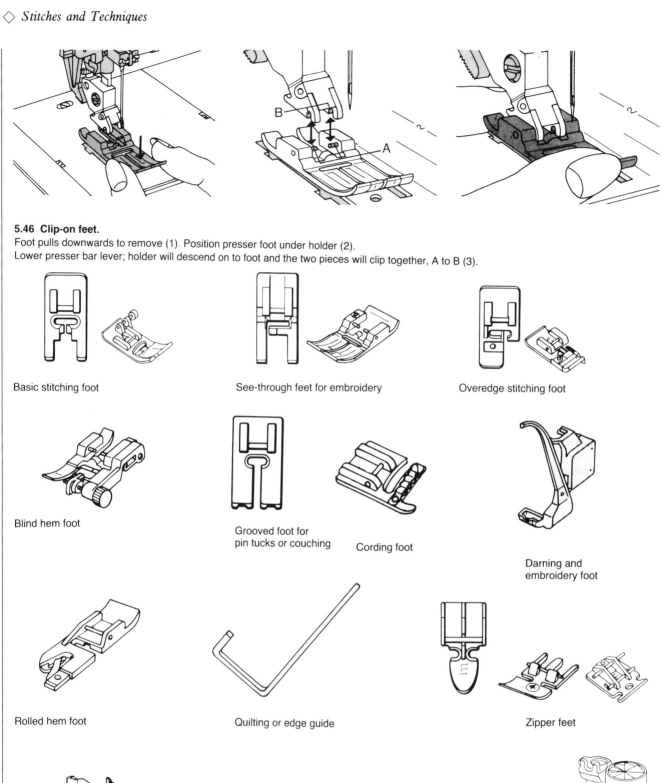

5.46 Clip-on feet.

Foot pulls downwards to remove (1). Position presser foot under holder (2).
Lower presser bar lever; holder will descend on to foot and the two pieces will clip together, A to B (3).

Basic stitching foot

See-through feet for embroidery

Overedge stitching foot

Blind hem foot

Grooved foot for
pin tucks or couching

Cording foot

Darning and
embroidery foot

Rolled hem foot

Quilting or edge guide

Zipper feet

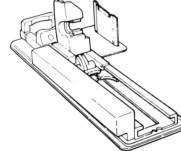

5.47 Examples of presser feet

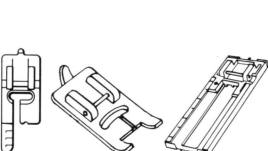

Buttonhole feet

◆ APPLIQUÉ

Appliqué is extensively used in fashion/dress, craft work, household items, children's clothes and toymaking. The term indicates the application by stitching of one fabric on to another in a (usually) decorative manner.

Lay the motif or design on to the base fabric, tack or pin and then stitch around the design with a decorative stitch. Satin stitch can be used, as can blanket or other craft stitch. Use the embroidery/clear plastic foot supplied to see the fabric edge clearly whilst sewing.

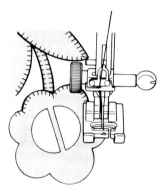

5.48 Appliqué

◆ BASTING

Basting is the American term for tacking. It is now the accepted universal term for machine tacking.

There are various methods. Some models have a stitch program, which means you just make your selection and the machine automatically produces the long tacking stitch; use the basic sewing foot (Bernina, Elna, Singer).

Another method is to select basting plus the basic stitch, and drop the feed dog; the machine will produce one stitch and stop. The operator pulls the fabric to the required position of the next stitch, depresses the pedal again and one more stitch is made. Work down the length to be tacked. The stitch can be as long or short as required.

One machine uses a special short basting needle (Necchi).

Alternatively, the longest straight stitch may be suitable.

◆ BLIND HEM

Blind hemming is designed for turning up hems on trousers, skirts, and curtains to give a secure finish. It is *not* invisible. On thick tweedy or bulked fabrics the stitches are less likely to show than the hem done on fine fabrics, where a small stitch is normally visible on the right side. Do not use on a very full skirt or bias cut garment. Use the blind hem foot supplied and follow the instructions in the illustration.

5.49 Appliqué
(New Home)

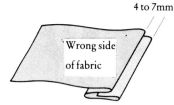

Light weight fabric

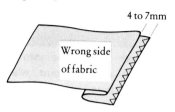

Heavy weight fabric

(1) On lightweight fabrics the raw edge can be turned under and pressed.
On heavyweight fabrics that ravel, the raw edge should be overcast first. Fold up the desired amount and pin in place. Then fold the hem under the fabric as illustrated.

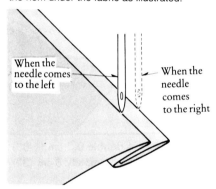

(2) Position the fabric so that the needle just pierces the folded part of the fabric when the needle comes over to the left side. Lower the presser foot.

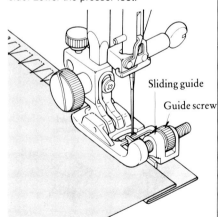

(3) Turn the guide screw and move the sliding guide next to the folded edge. Sew, guiding the folded edge along the sliding guide. For a professional looking hem, fold the fabric, reducing the lip to a scant 2 mm. As you sew, the right-hand stitch will fall off the fabric edge, forming a chain stitch.

5.50 Blind hemming

◆ BUTTONHOLES

Methods vary but are all successful. They can be described as semi-automatic, automatic, one-step (when the foot determines the size), memorized (on some computer machines) and sensor (two computer models have a sensor buttonhole foot).

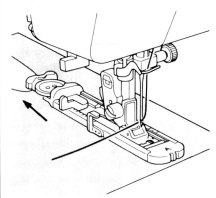

5.51 Example of a buttonhole foot, where the button is inserted to determine the length
(Jones & Brother)

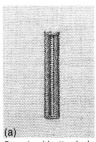 

(a) Standard buttonhole with bar-tacks

(b) Lingerie buttonhole

(c) Keyhole buttonhole

(d) Stretch buttonhole

(e) Rounded buttonhole

5.52 Examples of buttonholes

Machine setting

Buttonhole foot

(1) Always make a practice buttonhole on a scrap of fabric. Try the butonhole with the button you will use.

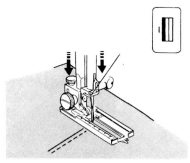

(2) Set the pattern selector dial as in the top right-hand corner of the diagram. Lead both threads to the left. Lower the needle into the fabric where the buttonhole is to start, and lower the foot.

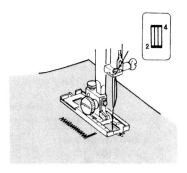

(4) Set the pattern selector dial as shown, and sew five stitches of bar-tack. Then raise the needle from the fabric.

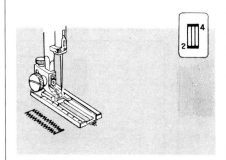

(6) Set the pattern selector dial as shown. Sew five stitches of bar-tack, and raise the needle from the fabric.

5.53 Automatic buttonholing

Automatic buttonholes

On the stitch selector of an automatic machine will be the buttonhole symbol. A buttonhole will be selected in the same way as any other stitch. The figure shows the format and stitch sequence in detail. When the buttonhole is completed the operator resets the dial at position 1 and repeats the process as required.

(3) Sew down the left side of the buttonhole to the bottom end.
Raise the needle.

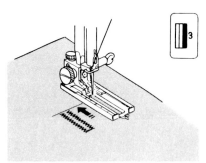

(5) Set the pattern selector dial as shown. Sew up the right side of the buttonhole. Stop the machine when you are directly opposite the first stitch on the left-hand side, and raise the needle.

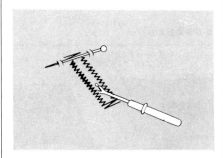

(7) Remove the fabric from the machine, and cut the sewing threads.
Insert a pin inside the bar-tack. Then cut the opening with a buttonhole cutter. Be careful not to cut the stitches.

5.54 Neat buttonhole foot for the memorized buttonhole
(Viking Husqvarna)

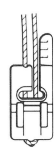

5.55 Corded buttonhole

One-step buttonholes

The button is placed into the buttonhole foot, and buttonhole is selected on the stitch selection panel. The machine will stitch the buttonhole at the size required for that button, stop and lock off. Alternatively the length is indicated by a sliding gauge on the foot, but the overall system is the same (Figure 5.51).

Memorized automatic buttonholes

Mark the length of the buttonhole. Select buttonhole. During the stitching of the desired size the machine is programmed in sequence by the operator. The machine will stop after the final bar-tack and lock off. The buttonhole is now in memory, and without further instruction the buttonhole sequence will be repeated until the machine is reprogrammed. Two different presser feet can be provided for this type of buttonhole: a slider foot, or a normal foot which is grooved on the underside to accommodate the lines of stitching.

In addition to the types of buttonhole mentioned, various models do have extra buttonhole features and some have preset memorized lengths.

Reinforced buttonholes

These can be sewn on some models by stitching around the sequence again but omitting the bar-tacks.

Corded buttonholes

These can be done on all machines. They look very professional, and in addition the buttonhole is strengthened. The cord is held on a hook at the back and front of the foot and the buttonhole stitches over the cord as the buttonhole is sewn in the normal way. When the buttonhole is complete, pull the cords to eliminate the loop. At the other end, take the cords to the reverse side and finish off by hand, or cut cords close to the end of the bar-tack (Figure 5.55).

Buttonholes should always be interfaced on every fabric, and it is advisable to do one or two test holes to check size and stitch density. Slit open with the buttonhole cutter.

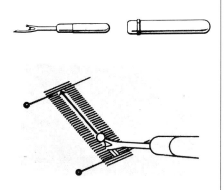

5.56 Cutting the buttonhole

◆ CORDING

The cording foot will hold up to three or more fine cords or threads. Because they are attached to the foot, the required design can be easily followed and the cords are perfectly placed. A variety of utility, craft or embroidery stitches can be sewn over the cords to couch them on to the base fabric. The basic design, the cord and the couching stitch and thread all contribute to the final effect.

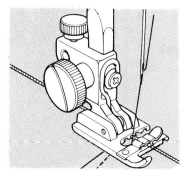

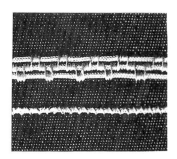

5.57 Cording: one and three threads couched

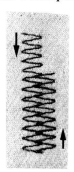

5.58 Tricot darning

 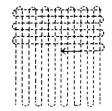

5.59 Two types of programmed darn sequences

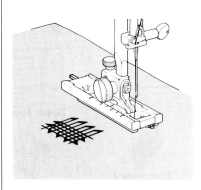

5.60 Programmed darn sequence with slider foot

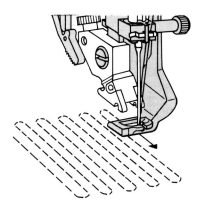

5.61 With the darning foot, machines can do a free darn of any size

◆ DARNING

Forwards and backwards stitching with tricot stitch provides a firm darn on most fabrics. By attaching the embroidery/darning foot and dropping the feed dog the traditional machine darn is achieved.

Specialist darn sequences are a feature of computer machines. In all instances, darn is selected and the machine will perform the stitch sequence and stop. If the area to be mended is large, move the fabric and repeat the darn sequence until the area is covered. For added strength it is recommended that a piece of lining or interfacing is placed behind the torn area.

◆ ELASTIC STITCHING

For swimwear, choose elastic that is specifically recommended. The best for the job is cotton braid swimwear elastic. This comes in a variety of widths and is usually sold by the yard off large spools. It is very durable; it retains its stretchability when stitched through and its shape when wet. Other elastics suitable for swimwear are polyester braid, nylon braid and polyester knit elastic. Avoid acetate elastic for swimwear; it loses its shape when wet, which means you may lose your suit! Be

5.63 Elastic stitching

sure to use the correct width of elastic as called for in the pattern instructions. Each width of elastic has a different amount of stretch and is not interchangeable without altering the fit of your suit.

Elastic strip is a newcomer on the haberdashery scene but is already popular. It is available in various widths. One or more rows of elastic can be used for ankles, cuffs, bodices and so on. The elastic is pulled out tight; the machine stitches rows of straight stitch *between* the elastic cords (and over the netting in between). When completed, the effect is the same as rows of shirring – but this technique is considerably easier!

5.62 Elastic stitching for swimwear (McCabe)

5.64 Faggotting

◆ FAGGOTTING

Faggotting is the joining of two pieces or strips of fabric with decorative stitching, but leaving a gap between the fabrics. The traditional method is to lay the pieces to be joined on to a base paper and tack or pin, so that during the stitching the paper holds the fabrics evenly spaced. Vilene Stitch-Tear can be substituted for the paper, and this works very well. Some machines provide a guide to keep the fabrics evenly spaced (Elna).

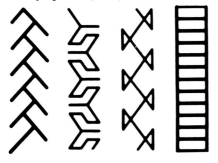

5.65 Faggotting stitches

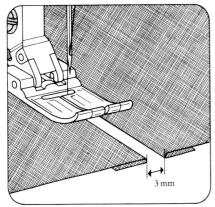

3 mm

5.66 Faggotting

5.67 Gathering (McCabe)

◆ GATHERING

Simple gathers are done with the basic foot and a long straight stitch. Sew two rows about 6–13 mm (¼ – ½ in) apart and then pull up both rows together with the bobbin thread. Some machines have a gathering foot supplied; follow the directions in the manufacturer's handbook. Usually this foot merely ensures a slackening of tension or a looser stitch.

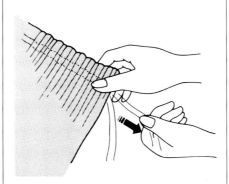

5.68 Pulling up gathers

◆ GATHERING WITH ELASTIC

This is a different type of gathering where the elastic is stitched on to the fabric for wrists, ankles, waist-lines, etc. Various types of elastic can be used depending on the finish required.

5.69 Gathering with elastic

Gathering with elastic (cont.)

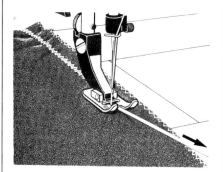

5.70 Zigzag stitch and cord

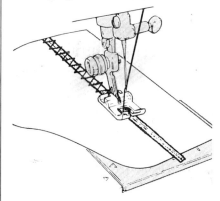

5.71 Tricot zigzag and knicker or flat elastic

◆ OVERLOCKING

We will use this term for all the 'seam and overcast' stitches. Various presser feet are supplied. Most incorporate a small wire prong; sometimes there are two or three prongs. When the stitch is sewn, the action of the needle passing the thread over the prongs will put extra thread into the stitch sequences so that the edges are less likely to buckle or pucker. This foot is used when the threads actually bind or oversew the *cut* edge.

Some overlock stitches – such as the knit stitch – sew not *over* the edge but *up* to it. The pronged foot would not be used in this instance as the stitch formation is different. Either an alternative overlocking foot is provided, or the normal presser foot can be used.

Various factors contribute to the finish obtained: fabric in use, thread, needle, type of stitch, type of machine and soon. No hard and fast rules can be given. However, if

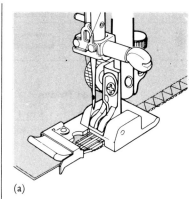

(a)

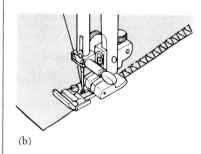

(b)

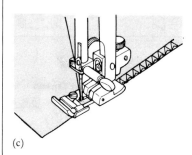

(c)

5.72 Samples of overlocking or overedging

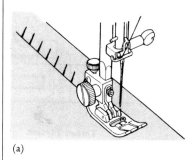

(a)

(b)

5.73 Knit stitch sewn on the seam line and trimmed afterwards

excessive puckering occurs, decrease the stitch *width*. An alternative is not to sew over the edge but to sew inside the edge of the seam allowance, that is to put the edge of the foot on the edge of the fabric; trim after stitching.

Opinions differ as to whether to trim the 16 mm (5/8 in) seam allowance in dressmaking before or after stitching. Again, there are no hard and fast rules; it depends on the stitch in use and the fabric. A test piece is required to decide which stitch is best suited to the job in hand, and this will determine whether the seam allowance is cut/ trimmed before or after stitching.

◆ PIN TUCKS

The traditional pin tuck is a tiny tuck about 3 mm (1/8 in) wide – usually sewn in rows for decoration. A machine that will move the *needle* into various stitching positions is an enormous help with this technique, because it is possible to move the needle to the stitching position required, thus determining the width of the tuck.

When stitching in this manner, put the edge of the foot on the edge of the fabric and move the needle to the required position. Alternatively, line the edge of the fabric with the centre slit in the presser foot and move the needle to the desired position. Mark the position of the tucks on the fabric. Press the first tuck, and stitch; press the second tuck, and stitch; and continue in this manner until the area to be tucked is completed.

See also twin-needle sewing later in this section.

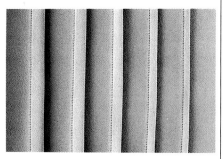

5.74 Pin tucks

◆ PIPING

Piping is the insertion of a thick cord into a bias cut strip of fabric. This is then inserted into a seam line for decorative purposes on dress, upholstery and various craft items. Use the zipper foot to make the piping strip and for insertion into the seam.

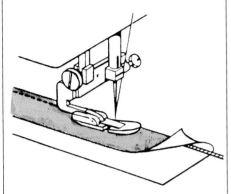

5.75 Making piping

5.76 Piping (McCabe)

◆ QUILTING

Quilted fabric is two or three layers sewn together, one of which is a wadding. It is usual to have the top fabric, then the wadding, and then either lining or interfacing on the bottom. Butter muslin is ideal as a backing/interfacing for this job on most fabrics. The fabrics must be well anchored together with tacking stitches. It is best to start stitching from the centre of the fabric and work out to each side. Mark the first

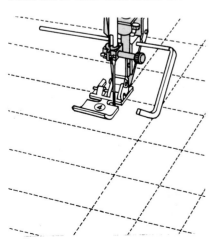

5.77 Quilting

5.78 Quilting (McCabe)

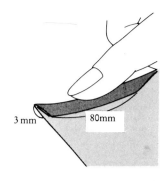

(1) Make a double 3 mm (1/8 in) fold about 80 mm in length.

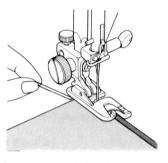

(2) Lower the needle into the fabric at the point where sewing is to begin, then lower the hemmer foot.

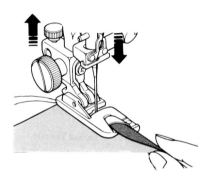

(3) Sew three or four stitches while holding the needle and bobbin threads. Lower the needle into the fabric and lift the hemmer foot. Insert the folded portion of the fabric into the curl of the hemmer foot.

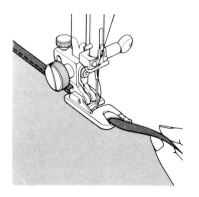

(4) Lower the hemmer foot, then sew by lifting up the edge of the fabric to keep it feeding smoothly and evenly. Straight stitch or zigzag can be used.

5.79 Rolled hemming

stitching line, then stitch; move the fabric across and place the quilting guide on the stitching line, then sew; move as before.

Quilting is most effective with decorative stitches rather than just the straight stitch, particularly on plain fabrics. It is simple to do but it does take a lot of thread, so remember to purchase extra reels.

Quilting is traditionally done in diamond shapes, but with modern interpretation it can be in squares. tramlines and other geometric styles. Using the darning/embroidery foot, it is possible to follow a design or pattern freely whilst quilting.

◆ ROLLED HEM

Even the most basic zigzag machine will come supplied with a rolled hem foot. It is not the most easy finish to perform, but the figure shows the sequence. Two tips are: to hold the two thread ends tightly and help pull through under the presser foot for the first few stitches; and to keep the fabric rolled in front of the foot and slightly pulled across to the left as the fabric feeds under the foot.

◆ SHELL TUCKS AND SHELL EDGING

This is an alternative edging for lingerie, babywear, and so on, and for use as a decorative finish. The fabric should be fine, such as crêpe de Chine or tricot. Use the blind hem stitch: the top tension is slightly tightened. Shell tucks are best sewn on the bias.

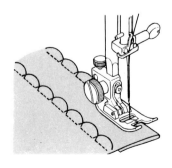

5.80 Shell tucks

5.81 Smocking (McCabe)

◆ SMOCKING

Smocking on the sewing machine is most effective. However, do *not* expect the exact, regimented stitches of the hand embroideress.

Machine smocking is creative and simple. The area to be smocked must be gathered by rows of stitching in the usual way. Stroke the gathers with a pin to ensure that they lie smoothly. A test piece will ascertain which of your stitches are most effective; satin and open embroidery stitches are suitable. Use the clear embroidery foot.

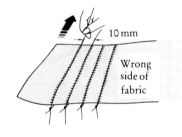

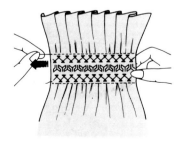

5.82 Smocking

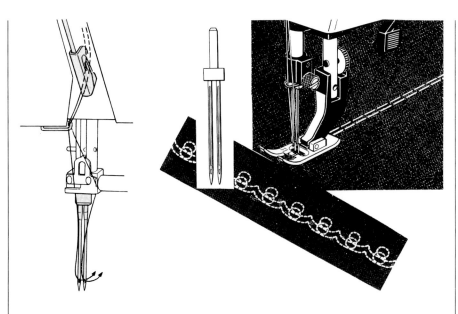

5.83 Twin-needle threading

5.84 Twin-needle stitching

5.86 Twin-needle tucking

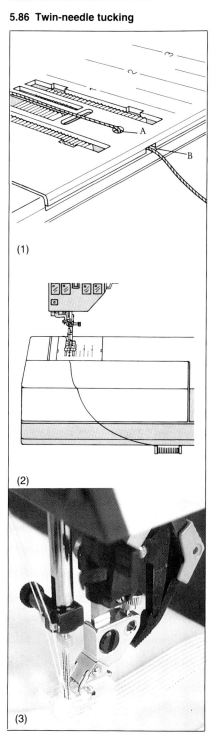

(1)

(2)

(3)

5.87 Twin-needle pin tucking with insertion cord

◆ TWIN-NEEDLE SEWING

Most automatic machines take a twin needle. This is two needles on one shank, which is inserted into the machine in the normal manner. Thread the machine with two reels of thread of matching or contrast colours. There is still only *one* bobbin thread, and it can be a good idea to match this thread to the fabric if two contrasting top threads are being used. Use the normal presser foot except when tucking. The twin-needle control should be used if there is one on the machine. This reduces the needle swing to ensure that the second needle does not hit the presser foot.

Top stitching

Two identical rows of top stitching are possible for jeans and fashion garments.

Embroidery stitching

Embroidery stitches of all kinds can be used for a variety of decorative effects.

Twin-needle tucking

It the bottom (bobbin) tension is tightened considerably, a tucked effect will be obtained. This is particularly nice on jersey fabrics or soft cottons or lawn. Use a grooved foot if tucks are very close together.

Twin-needle tucking with insertion cord

The tucks are obtained in the same way as for twin-needle tucking. Before stitching, insert a cord through the needle plate of the machine. As the machine stitches, the cord is automatically fed into the back of the tuck. This provides an extremely attractive finish with a pronounced ridged effect. Machines without the hole in the needle plate often provide an alternative method to hold the cord – see your manufacturer's handbook.

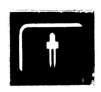

5.85 Examples of twin-needle control buttons

Decorative hem stitching

Decorative hem stitching is particularly beautiful using the twin-wing needle. Use this needle in the normal twin-stitching way and select the required stitch. Many models have special hem stitches.

Hem stitching is a craft technique and should not be confused with turning hems on garments.

5.88 Twin-wing needle

◆ ZIPPERS

Zipper feet vary. However, on the latest machines it is usual to have a clip-on foot because the sliding type is not necessary when the needle position can be moved. The foot can clip on in left, right or centre positions too. Zipper feet, therefore, are

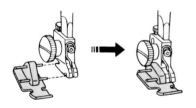

To sew the left side of the zipper, attach the zipper foot to the pin on the right-hand side.

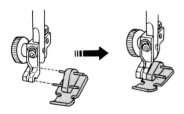

To sew the right side of the zipper, attach the zipper foot to the pin on the left-hand side.

5.89 Clip-on zipper feet

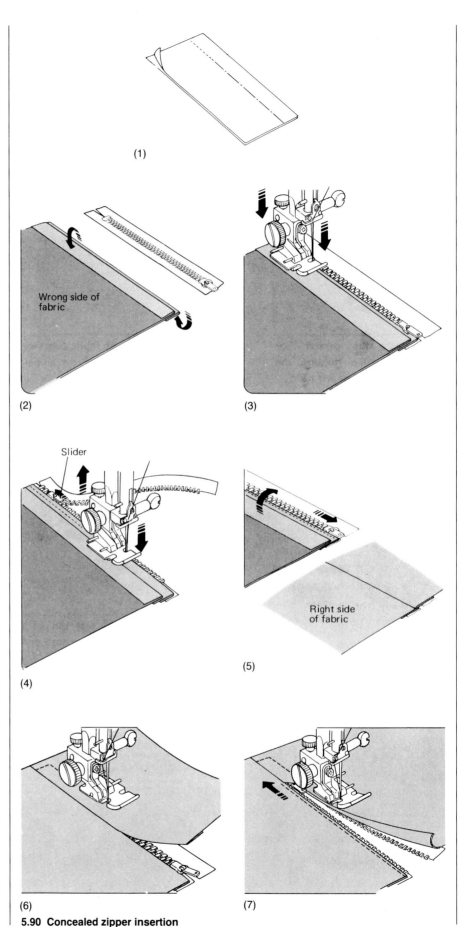

5.90 Concealed zipper insertion

much smaller and neater than their predecessors. They do vary in basic shape somewhat, but all do the job successfully.

Concealed zipper insertion

This is the traditional way to insert a zip into a skirt or trousers with a side opening or with a fly front.

To prepare the fabric, place the right sides together and sew to the end of the zipper opening (1). Reverse stitch to knot the stitches. Sew the zipper opening with basting stitches.

To insert the zip, fold back the left seam allowance. Turn under the right seam allowance to form a 0.2 to 0.3 cm (1/8 in) fold. Place the zipper teeth next to the fold and pin in place (2).

Lower the needle into the fabric at the point where sewing is to begin, then lower the foot (3). Sew through fold and zipper tape. Stop just before the zipper foot reaches the slider on the zipper tape (4). Turn the balance wheel by hand and lower the needle into the fabric. Raise the zipper foot and open the zipper. Lower the foot and stitch the remainder of the seam.

Close the zipper and spread the fabric flat with the right side facing up (5). Move the zipper foot to the left pin (6). Guide the edge of the foot along the zipper teeth and stitch through garment and zipper tape. Stop about 5 cm (2 in) from the top of the zipper.

With the needle down in the fabric, raise the foot, remove the basting stitches and open the zipper (7). Then lower the foot and stitch the remainder of the seam, making sure the fold is even.

Semi-concealed zipper insertion

For a long back zip or a centre front opening on a dress or tunic, the concealed zip opening will give the same amount of overlap each side of the teeth.

To prepare the fabric, place the right sides of the fabric together and

sew to the end of the zipper opening. Reverse stitch to knot the stitches. Sew the zipper opening with basting stitches. Open out and press.

Insert the zip as follows. With zipper foot against the teeth of the zip, stitch down, across and up the other side. Take great care when stitching *across* the zipper not to break the needle. Nylon and polyester zips will sew easily here, but metal zippers can prove a problem.

Fly front zipper

Iron the fly edge. Baste the closed zipper underneath the pressed right-hand fly edge so that its teeth are still visible. Pin facing strip A to the underside and stitch it down at the same time as you sew on the zipper. The zipper teeth move along the right-hand guide edge (1). Shortly before you reach the end of the seam, leave the needle down in the material, raise the sewing foot and open the zipper. Then lower the foot again and sew the seam to the end. Close the zipper.

Fold the right edge over the left and pin it in place according to the seam line. Then baste in the left zipper chain (2).

Open the zipper. Attach the edge guide and adjust it so that its finger moves along the fabric edge (3). Shortly before you reach the end of the seam, leave the needle down in the material, raise the sewing foot and close the zipper. Then lower the foot again and sew to the end of the seam. Secure the end of the zipper seam with a tack.

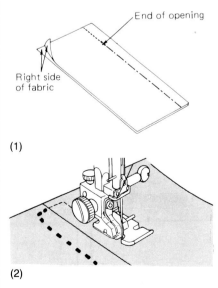

(1)

(2)

5.91 Semi-concealed zipper insertion

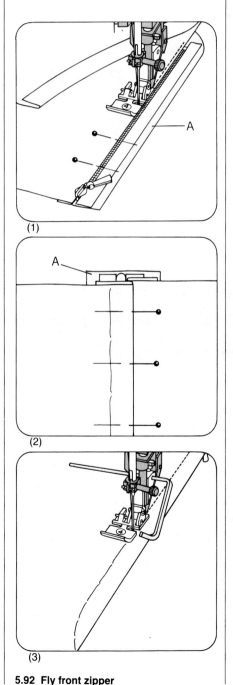

(1)

(2)

(3)

5.92 Fly front zipper

Invisible zippers

The zipper foot included with some New Home machines is designed to stitch normal and invisible zippers. Pfaff will supply an invisible zipper foot on request. Invisible zipper feet (universal) are available (Figure 5.93).

Invisible zippers are available at larger department stores. This type of zipper is suitable for all fabrics from fine silk crêpe de Chine and silky jerseys to suit-weight wools and tweeds, and can be inserted into skirts, trousers, dresses and so on. The opening is totally invisible on the right side of the garment and looks like another seam.

To insert a zip, use the following sequence. Remember – the zipper is laid on the *right* side (outside) of the garment.

Do not sew the seam below the zip. Open the zipper and lay the left side on the garment (1), with the teeth on the seam line (usually 16 mm 5/8 in) inside the fabric edge) and the top of the zipper opening approximately 6 mm (1/4 in) below the waist/neck seam line. Pin into place with pins at 90 degrees to the zip.

With zipper foot or normal presser foot, sew the zip into place on the outside edge of the tape (2).

Using the invisible zipper foot, sew the stitching line under the teeth, with the needle in the central hole and the teeth under the left-hand tunnel (3). When the foot reaches the zip pull/tag, either lock off or do one or two reverse stitches to fasten off.

Repeat steps 1–3 on the right-hand side of the tape and garment, using the right-hand tunnel on the foot (4).

Close the zip. Lay out the garment and pin or tack the seam from hem line to zipper. Stitch from the hem upwards towards the zip on the seam line, using the zipper foot with the needle on the right-hand outside of the foot. When you reach the zipper continue sewing alongside the previous stitching line for 13–19 mm (1/2–3/4 in) and then lock off. This overlap is vital so that there is no poke at the bottom of the zip in wear.

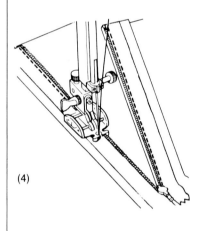

(1)　　(2)

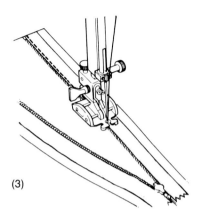

(3)

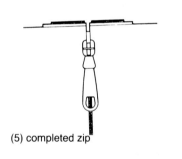

(5) completed zip

(4)

5.93 Invisible zipper insertion

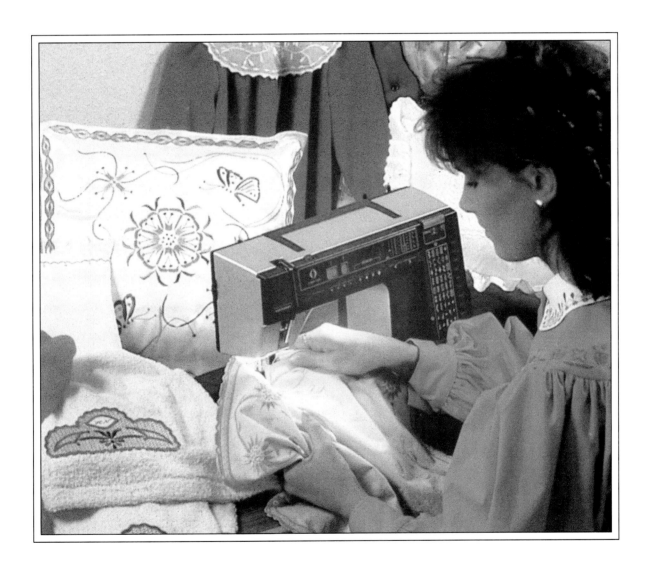

FINISHING TOUCHES

Without question the most important contributions to a professional finish – whether in fashion or sewing for the home – are the choices made at the very beginning of the project:

◇ Colour
◇ Fabric
◇ Drape and texture of the fabric
◇ Choice of pattern/style of curtain etc.

If any of these combinations are wrong then the finished article will be less than perfect.

During the making up the following also contribute to an excellent finish:

◇ Exact cutting of the fabric.
◇ Transferring construction points exactly.
◇ Exact matching during construction and stitching.
◇ Checking measurements (fitting as appropriate) at each stage.
◇ Pressing everything that is stitched *as you go along*.
◇ Never cutting corners.

Outward signs of a good finish are, for example:

◇ Tidy work.
◇ Symmetrical details, such as lapel points and pocket flaps matching exactly.
◇ Pattern and stripes matching.
◇ Well-set shoulders.

A superb outfit will be completed with couture details such as saddle stitching, rouleau loops, covered buttons and buckles, and matching ties or scarves. First-class household sewing will include exactly toning fringes and trims, curtain tie-backs, monogrammed towels and linen, and so on. Finishing touches become the signature of the person making up, and signify not just a professional job but also personal style and taste.

Sewing machines are excellently equipped to contribute to the perfection of finish, whether it be by embellishment or just by being able to cope correctly with the extra needs for finishing the outfit or room setting – from leather to silk, from picot edge to curtain headings, from the blazer badge to the monogrammed pillow. From the moment you choose to make anything, plan the finishing touches you can do on the machine with as much care as you would the other accessories such as shoes, bag and beads, or light fittings, pictures and ornaments.

Throughout this book we have moved in easy stages through choosing styles and colours, considering textures, working through patterns and understanding stitches and techniques for the 1001 projects that can be tackled. We now look at some ideas for finishing in fashion and home sewing.

FASHION FINISH

To illustrate fashion finish we first show two designer outfits – made from couture commercial patterns – which have been accessorized in two different ways. In this era of busy living we need our clothes to have double lives and to take us anywhere. After all, we have put a great deal into their making up!

We then go on to look at other fashion ideas.

◆ THREE-PIECE WOOL OUTFIT

The three-piece outfit is made in Liberty Veruna wool and matching wool crêpe. The trousers, top and flowing duster coat are super as a matching outfit. However, they can all be interchangeable in a mix-and-match wardrobe using the green and black as the basic colour scheme.

Despite the designer label, the garments are easy to make and the outfit is basically unstructured. Hems, cuffs, necklines and bands are all narrow and finished with top stitching. The secret to a crisp, smart and professional finish is to top stitch and then *edge* stitch.

By changing tights, shoes, beads and other accessories and mixing and matching with other garments in the colour field, a distinctly different effect can be obtained – as you can see from the photographs.

6.1 Two ways of accessorizing the Liberty veruna outfit to suit the occasion (McCabe)

◆ TWO-PIECE MOHAIR SUIT

The two-piece, tweed, mohair suit is a classic of its kind. Very much at home in town or country, business or socializing, it can take you anywhere.

This type of fabric needs greater care when handling than a more stable weave. When cutting out it should be carefully positioned so that the fibres are not distorted and pulled out of alignment. Grain lines are particularly important with a more open weave, and never more than when the fabric also includes a check. All the construction symbols must be carefully aligned so that the checks meet at exactly the right spot on both skirt and jacket. Failure here will result in a very unacceptable finish.

When you are making up, the fabric must be carefully married to its counterpart so that – again – checks meet and the fabric is not stretched in stitching. Place pins at right angles to the stitching line to hold the fabric securely in position.

Overcasting (overlocking) is vitally important so that the fabric does not fray during making up and wear. All sewing machines will neaten – from zigzag through to overcasting stitches – but an overlocker will do the job very quickly and easily.

Pressing is always important, but exceptionally so in this type of soft tailoring. Press as you go, with a damp cloth and the very toe (point) of the iron: do not stretch during pressing.

For a particular emphasis the red of the suiting fabric was picked out for the lining fabric – a heavy polyester faille. The scope for accessories is wide: black, red and a variety of the little specks of colour can be picked out and accentuated for special effect. The pictures show the suit in both formal and more casual manner; the effects are obtained by the choice of accessories.

6.2 Tweed mohair suit accessorized for fromal and informal wear (McCabe)

◆ EMBROIDERED EVENING DRESS

Many commercial patterns have areas that can be embellished to good effect. It can be an excellent design feature to embroider yokes, sleeves and cuffs. If you have a particular favourite dress or blouse you can cut your own pieces to insert, providing you follow the basic construction lines and remember to *add* seam allowances.

1 Sketch the design on to pattern pieces.
2 Transfer them to the fabric. If a particularly delicate fabric is used, trace with a tacking line.
3 Mount the fabric on to an underlining if a sheer or very delicate fashion fabric is being used.
4 Place on Stitch-and-Tear and stitch.
5 To give extra definition and texture to the design, place a thin layer of wadding or domett behind the fashion fabric. Lay them on to butter muslin and stitch.
6 Make up the dress – the usual way, following the pattern instructions.

6.3 Embroidered evening dress (Viking)

◆ EMBROIDERED KNITS

Embroidered jumpers are fashion news. Either personalize a ready-to-wear bargain, or design your own original, combining your skills in knitting and on the sewing machine.

Silk floss was used for the child's jersey pattern, with pearl beads added for extra interest.

1 Use a bold pattern, a bold colour and a bold heavy thread which will show up well.
2 Sketch the pattern with a vanishing pen, or mark with a loose tacking thread.
3 Use a Teflon needle and light pressure on the presser foot. A walking foot or roller foot will be useful.

6.4 Child's embroidered jersey (Elna)

◆ APPLIQUÉD JUMPERS

Appliqué on jumpers can add interest and texture. It can also update last year's purchase into this year's fashion – or transform a plain jumper into something quite exotic, with lurex threads and satin and sparkle for an evening sweater with a difference.

1 Plan the design and draw to scale.
2 Cut out pieces in tissue or Vilene and use as pattern pieces when cutting fabric.
3 If the pieces are likely to fray a lot, fuse them on to very soft interfacing.
4 Pin and tack in place, building up the design as required.
5 Stitch with satin stitch or other suitable fancy pattern.
6 Finish off with detail embroidery and/or beads and sequins as required.

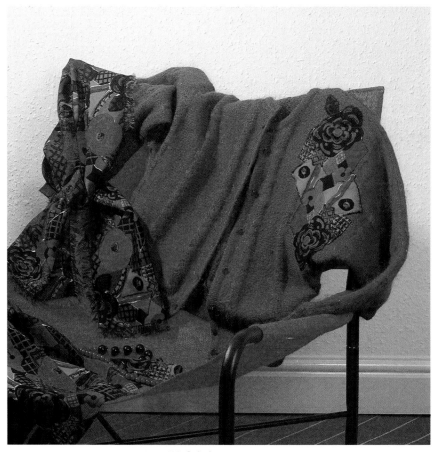

6.5 Appliquéd cardigan by Myra (McCabe)

◆ EMBROIDERED COLLAR

Separate collars are a fashion feature, and so need to stand out. They must be crisp; lawn, piqué and poplin are favourites, as they can be starched. A more luxurious look is obtained by using organdie – as in our design.

1 Self-coloured embroidery looks extra special and expensive.
2 The stitches need supporting with Stitch-and-Tear or vanishing muslin.
3 Work the scalloped edge *before* cutting; that is, stitch at the width of the presser foot inside the edge of the collar. Trim close to the stitching.
4 Bind the neck edge for strength in wear.

◆ DECORATIVE ZIP CLOSURES

Whilst care is usually taken to conceal a zipper – either by lapping the fabric or by using an invisible zip – there are occasions when a feature zip can add interest to the design.

1 Use a zip of contrasting colour, and merely show the teeth and tape for an easy finish.
2 Trim the edge of the opening with braid or embroidery to highlight this design feature. Colours can be contrasted to or co-ordinated with the zip and fabric.
3 Heavier trims, pipings, braids, cords and threads will usually team best with a decorative zipper insertion, particularly when using chunky plastic or metallic teeth.
4 Add a decorative tassel, fob, ring or bead to the hole in the puller for a final touch of flair.

6.6 Embroidered collar (Viking)

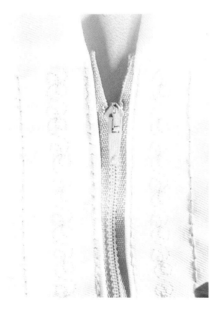

6.7 Decorative zipper matching zipper and embroidery thread (McCabe)

BRIDAL AND LINGERIE

The techniques and stitches in bridal and lingerie sewing go hand in hand, because the fabrics used are very similar. Sumptuous, luscious, slippery and silky, they can all prove exquisite problems!

Getting a good finish on a difficult fabric is not as hard as it would first appear. The secret is usually in handling the fabric properly and then in using correct stitches, thread and needles.

If the fabric stretches out of shape it is a good idea to lay the pieces on to an ironing board with a padded surface so that they can be anchored in their exact shape whilst pinning or tacking. This is suitable for very slippery fabrics too.

Pin at right angles to the seam lines to keep the fabric firmly in position. Whilst stitching, do not pull the fabric out of shape. Let the machine take the material through at its own speed; do not pull from behind or stretch the fabric in front of the needle.

Refer to Parts 2 and 4 for advice on lining and interlining fabrics of certain types. This is particularly important with wedding gowns, so that they hang correctly and do not embarrass the bride by showing too much flesh through a flimsy fabric.

Traditionally, all seams on voiles, chiffons, organza, organdie and similar fabrics, were stitched with French seams. This is still a correct technique, but the modern sewing machine will provide a variety of overlocking and overcasting stitches which can be just as neat – and sometimes neater!

The basic satin stitch, or picot edgings, can prove a boon for frills, flounces, hemlines and sleeves on sheer fabrics. Use them: they look very good! Lace application is straightforward: lots and lots of lace looks both feminine and expensive.

Ribbon is an excellent foil for trimmings, but matching rouleau can give an extra special finish.

Use rouleau for button loops, frog fastenings and straps and bows.

6.9 **Trousseau by Maggie Swain** (McCabe)

1 Take a length of fabric 1 in wide and of the desired length: it must be cut on the cross (on the bias).
2 Fold in half – do not press – and pin to secure, right side to the inside.
3 Stitch down the centre of the strip.
4 With a rouleau loop turner (or bodkin as a second best alternative) pull one end down through the sausage and turn the whole length inside out.

5 It is important not to trim the seam allowance before turning: it is this extra fabric that makes the rouleau nice and round. Do not press. Use as required.

6.10 **Lace appliqué** (McCabe)

6.11 **Lingerie** (McCabe)

BADGES AND MOTIFS

◆ BADGES

Use traditional felt for badges: it is a very stable fabric. Apply an iron-on Vilene or cotton interfacing to the back for a crisp finish and cut edge. Draw the design shape and centre points with a vanishing pen; the marks fade, or can be easily removed with damp. Badges should be bright and striking, so use vivid colours.

6.12 Blazer badge (Elna)

◆ APPLIQUÉ AND EMBROIDERY

For the jacket shown, appliqué and embroidery have been built up directly on to the front. The birds, moon, stars, fish and trees are all preselected designs on the machine. *Before* making up the garment, sketch the design on to fabric with vanishing pen. Appliqué the fabric pieces, embroider the motifs, and then construct the garment. A ready-to-wear garment could be similarly embellished.

6.13 Appliquéd jacket (Elna)

◆ PICTOGRAMS

On the machine illustrated, 15 satin stitch segments are available to be programmed into suitable sequences for the chosen design. Here we show the application of pictograms to his-and-hers holiday shirts.

The design is gradually built up, the top thread colours being changed as required. Use the bobbin thread in a shade matching the back ground material.

Use double fabric for the pockets, and Stitch-and-Tear on the sleeves. Use Sylko Supreme or embroidery cotton on a garment that needs ironing not a polyester thread.

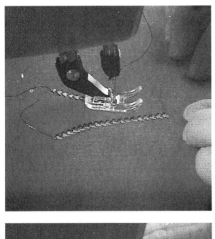

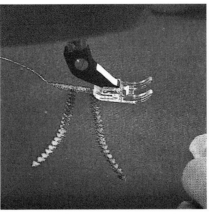

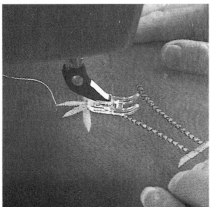

6.14 Building up pictograms (Viking)

ACCENT ON ACCESSORIES

Accessories are a very important part of the finished outfit, whether it is formal or casual, and for a man, woman or child! The modern machine offers a wealth of decorative stitches or specialist techniques to finish off these items. It must be remembered, however, that on many occasions a simple matching bag, belt, scarf or handkerchief is all that is required.

◆ SCARF FRINGING

Fringing for scarves is simple and extremely effective. Choose a lightweight, soft wool with a medium to loose weave! Veruna or challis is ideal. Cut the fabric to size – usually square or long and narrow.

Pull a single thread from each side of the scarf to the measured depth of the fringe. Using this pulled thread as a guide, stitch with a toning thread. Use either the straight stretch stitch or the traditional buttonhole stitch on stitch width 1 or 2. Make sure that the stitch swings into the scarf, *not* into the edging!

After stitching, pull out all the remaining threads from the edge of the scarf. You will be left with a very secure and attractively finished fringe.

6.15 Fringed scarf: Liberty veruna wool by Myra (McCabe)

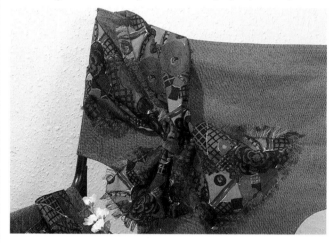

◆ TIES

Ties can be made from a variety of fabrics – fine wool, soft cotton, Vyella, and of course pure silk. It is recommended that a commerical pattern is purchased because the cut of the tie is crucial for successful tying. The tie must be cut in two pieces, and these on the cross. It is also important to interface correctly. However, do not be afraid to try tie making as it is quite straightforward.

Personalize the tie by embroidering it with initials or a motif or logo. The ultimate finish is to embroider the owner's own signature; this is possible on a free-programming machine. A matching handkerchief will finish the effect nicely.

◆ BAGS

Purses, pouches and bags come in all shapes, sizes and types of fabric. If it enhances the outfit, anything goes!

When making bags, bear in mind the type of use they will get and construct them accordingly. For example, a tote bag or sports bag will need much greater strength of fabric, thread and closure than a purely decorative evening bag.

6.16 Beautiful bags: patchwork, leather and velvet by Myra (McCabe)

For strength use a buttonhole twist or bold thread or a very strong cotton which has been waxed. For stitch strength use the straight stretch stitch; no stretch is required, but the reverse (back) stitch will give exceptional strength.

For decoration use the usual array of cotton, polyester, embroidery and metallic threads. Closures can vary from the straightforward tie of tape, braid or ribbon to buckles and professional twist fasteners (these can be purchased from leather suppliers).

Linings are important; a decorative bag can be enhanced by a decorative lining. Either embroider the lining fabric or use something that is rather lush or expensive looking; a bag is usually quite small, so a modest piece of fabric is all that is required. To give the bag more substance it is a good idea to quilt the lining. A layer of wadding between the lining material and a fine butter muslin is sufficient.

A travel bag, beach bag or cosmetic bag is usefully lined with a waterproof material: shower curtaining is ideal for this. If the water-

6.18 Holiday bag: Liberty linen by Myra (McCabe)

proofing is transparent it can be interlined with a pretty fabric for good effect.

A mixture of embroidery and appliqué is used on the motif of a crocodile on the schoolbag. The shape of the cut-out exactly matches the little embroidery motifs. With the wide range of flowers, animals, trains and so on now available on machines, this idea is easily copied.

1 Heavy linen is ideal for children's bags, as it can be washed. Choose compatible fabrics for appliqué designs and background/bag material.
2 Draw the design on to fabric; back with fusible Vilene.
3 Stitch the little alligator motifs in lines, spaced at the width of the presser foot.
4 Cut out the large alligator shape.
5 Appliqué the cut-out on to the bag flat with a secure stitch: the traditional blanket stitch is used here.

6.17 Appliquéd schoolbag (Elna)

◆ TRIMS

Detachable trims for shoes, brooches, hair slides and so on can be made from a huge variety of materials. Lace, ribbon, leather, beads and sequins contribute to the desired effect. The easiest way to follow fashion here is to study the stores and just copy whatever you see on the counters!

The flower-heads illustrated are just petal shapes drawn out, stitched around and layered in the desired number. This is simple but extremely effective.

6.19 Flower trims (Bernina)

CRAFTS FOR CHILDREN

6.20 'Emeline': dressed in Liberty Jubilee by Maggie Swain. Below: detail of petticoat stitching (McCabe)

◆ DOLLS' CLOTHES

Toymaking, dolls and their dressing and embellishment is a dedicated craft and great fun to do. There is also a lot of skill and patience required for those tiny seams and armholes etc!

◇ Use the free arm for greater manipulation of tiny items. Needle movement will also be a great asset.

◇ Use tiny prints on fabrics to keep the proportion of the doll correct. Use soft fabrics for dresses and petticoats; any stiffness at all will be emphasized in miniature. Use fine needles (such as 11 scarfed) on the materials and trims.

◇ Commercial patterns are available for dolls and dolls' clothes, and both inexperienced and confident sewers will find them invaluable.

◇ Use elastic strip, cord elastic and 1/4 in knicker elastic on tiny items. Apply with tricot stitch, or make a tiny casing of zigzag. Ribbons and trims should be kept in proportion to the garment; many types are available. So too are tiny hooks, eyes and pops – but tiny fingers may find a small Velcro fastener easier to manipulate.

◇ Plain cottons and lawns can be embroidered to exceedingly good effect. Many techniques such as tucks, shell edging, faggotting and lace insertion are put to excellent use on the traditional doll.

◇ Stuff the dolls well – particularly the neck!

◆ RAGBOOKS

Ragbooks are super educational playthings, and very good fun to make. Ideally they should be in a washable fabric – cotton or polycotton – so that they can be thrown in the washing machine. Of course, any scraps of material can be used to give texture and added interest if laundering is not intended.

1 Treat each page as a separate picture. Then stitch two together, back to back, to form a page.
2 Punch eyelets (purchase on the haberdashery counter) or make eyelets on the machine. Tie the pages together with lace or ribbon.
3 Appliqué characters and story items. Quilt to give added dimension.
4 Finishing touches are pockets that open, buttons that undo, zips that will move, and so on; these will delight little fingers.

6.21 Ragbook (New Home)

HOME MAKING

6.22 Fabrics in the home (McCabe)

The choice of fabrics for curtains, upholstery, cushions and blinds is excellent. From exquisite sheers to lively cottons and linens, mix and match fabrics and friezes with wallpapers too, and on to the heavy velvets, flocks and embossed satins: every home can have its own distinctive decor.

Finishing touches in home making include the additional touch of colour to spice the whole arrangement; the piped cushion rather than the plain seam; the invisible zipper rather than the bulky closure; and extra fullness in curtains and drapes, and superb pleated heading tapes. Match tiebacks for the curtains, and take time to add a frill or pelmet; transform a plain blind into a work of art with appliqué or embroidery; make a lampshade; personalize towels and bed linen with monograms; and make tablecloths or table-mats with matching napkins. Finally, an extra touch of quilting, embroidery, tucking or patchwork can transform a plain or shop-bought item and place it squarely into the centre of your room scheme.

The basic techniques for piping, quilting and so on have been described in Part 5.

◆ QUILTING

Quilting very large items can be a problem if you have a small machine with little room between the base plate and the machine head! It is as well to think of this. It can be a good idea to make the cover in sections and then piece these together at the end. Wadding seems very thick until it is actually stitched down, especially for bedding; so use a heavier wadding than you first think is required!

Whilst tramline quilting is very effective, there are alternatives. A plain fabric is attractive quilted with an embroidery stitch; this is quick to do, but it eats a lot of thread. A patterned fabric is quilted to good effect with saddle stitch instead of the ordinary straight stitch. If you have a large all-over floral it is most interesting to quilt around the flower patterns.

◆ FRILLS

The addition of a frill will always soften the line of the item being trimmed and give a more feminine appearance. Keep the frill in the right proportion: roll or 1/4 in flat hem the edge before stitching it in place.

It is usual for a really full frill to allow twice the length of the item being trimmed; one and a half times the length is the very minimum you can get away with. Stitch two lines of gathers because this pulls up more evenly, and pull the underneath threads (bobbin threads) for a better finish.

6.23 and 6.24 Mix 'n' match fabrics used to excellent effect for bedroom (McCabe)

◆ BATHROOMS

Bathrooms can be planned to be functional and austere or feminine and pretty! Personalized towels can fit into either decorative scheme. Depending on your machine there are various ways of providing monograms but on terry toweling a simple satin stitch will usually be best – the lettering can be as stylized as you wish.

Keep curtains and blinds in the bathroom to a fabric that is easily laundered – cottons, polycottons, lace and so on. Simple and effective is the lace drape. Put a pole across the window – either inside or outside the frame – and merely hang the lace over the pole. Your fabric should be 1½–2 times the width of your window and 3 times the drop in length. Arrange the lace over the pole and pull to each side, securing with tie backs of lace or ribbon. Lace is now available very wide (72 in and more) with attractive scalloped edges; all the sewing necessary is to hem the bottom ends!

6.25 Pretty curtains and monogrammed towels – simple ways to personalize your bathroom by Myra (McCabe)

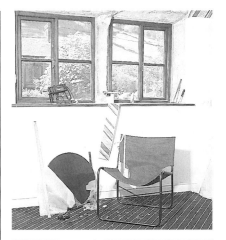

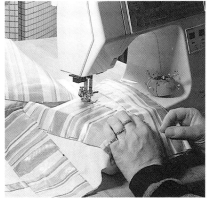

6.26a Sewing the pieces (McCabe)

b After: chair and cushion complement the curtains and freize (McCabe)

◆ IDEAS FOR FABRIC PIECES

With the necessity to match the pattern drops on a figured fabric and to get the exact width for the type of heading tape being used, there is always a certain amount of fabric left over from curtain projects. These pieces can be of varying size, and it is certainly a great pity to waste any.

Some pieces will be large enough for cushion covers – if only one side. Some will be ideal for frills and piping for trimming cushions and covers. Little pieces can be used for patchwork and appliqué for cushions and even trimming chairs and table-cloths. Flower heads cut out from the design are focal points when stitched on to plain fabric – and the contrasting fabric of a piping will also be eye-catching. Log cabin patchwork is an ideal medium for the sewing machine (all straight lines!) and strip or ribbon patchwork or appliqué can be top stitched into position.

A purchased chair can be enlivened with a motif to match the curtains. Alternatively, a similar chair or director's chair can be purchased and recovered in matching fabric.

Cushions can be fun and interesting to make. Lots of small cushions will give comfort combined with a lot of decorative ideas, and can be an inexpensive feature.

6.27 Mix 'n' match cushions using various techniques by Myra (McCabe)

TABLE LINEN

6.28 Christmas tablecloth (McCabe)

6.29 Cross-stitch border design (Pfaff)

Table-cloths have been out of fashion, but are now regaining something of their former glory. A variety of finishes and embroideries can make them suitable for casual breakfasts or more formal occasions.

Table-mats, tray-cloths and centrepieces are also decorative additions to the dining room. They can follow your colour scheme for the room.

With the renewed interest in Edwardian furniture and cottagey furnishings, there is also a place in the modern home for little mats and cloths dotted around on dressing tables, chests and other featured furniture.

A Christmas table-cloth can be a bright centrepiece for the festivities – and a new heirloom! The motifs illustrated can be found on the Singer sew-ware cartridges. When the size of the table-cloth is determined, purchase either a ready-made cloth or the correct size of fabric, which can be straight hemmed or hem stitched.

Cut out some circles of paper to represent the motifs and place them on the cloth to determine the desired effect and exact placement: mark with a vanishing pen or chalk. Stitch the motifs in the desired positions. Similar festive designs can be performed with free embroidery, or by building up designs with the stitches and embroidery designs in automatic or computer machines.

Hem stitching is a traditional

6.30 Hemstitching

6.31 Gold threads match the China (Elna)

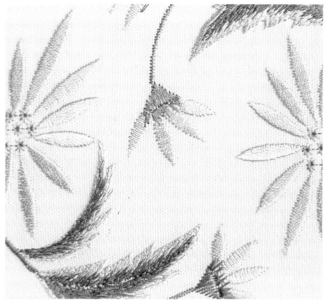

6.32 Traditional floral embroidery (New Home)

hand finish for both table and bed linen. It is extremely effective and easy to perform on a machine with a wing needle or twin-wing needle. Draw the number of threads for the required hem-stitch width. Turn the hem, placing the edge alongside the drawn threads. Stitch using a traditional buttonhole stitch. For decorative borders of hem stitching, threads can be drawn; or, if the fabric is fine enough, the piercing of the wing needle alone can show the holes in the design. Most fully automatic or computer machines have suitable stitches, such as honeycomb, ladder and picot.

Cross-stitch is yet another traditional finish for linen. It is available on many makes of machine, and traditional or modern motifs and borders can be designed to suit all types of taste and decor.

Embroidered flowers and foliage have always been favourite table linen decoration. Computer machines will allow elongation of petal shapes so that various sizes can be stitched to perfection. Good use of colour and the filler stitches will fill in the foliage and background shapes. The preselectable stem stitches will complete the design quickly and effectively.

That special, lovingly created gift is always treasured. For a unique touch, you can copy the design of your china. Gold or silver threads are available for machine sewing, and many can be laundered. Build up your design with preprogrammed stitches; if you have a machine that does free programming, the design can be copied in exact detail.

Lace trimming is a quick way to finish off a cloth for any type of use. Apply lace as an edging, or insert a motif or strips around the border. This is also an ideal way to use old lace: reapply it to new fabric. Lay the lace on to the fabric, and pin or tack. Stitch using either plain satin stitch or a very close buttonhole stitch. Trim away the fabric under the lace *after* stitching for a secure, smooth finish. Do not try to stitch the edge of the lace to the edge of the cloth; it will pucker and fray. Care must be taken to raise the presser foot and turn the fabric around the points in the lace rather than to steer around the corners: this ensures that the lace design is not stretched.

6.33 Re-apply old lace to new fabric by Myra (McCabe)

BLINDS

6.34 Sheer, decorated roller blind (Elna)

Soft, pretty blinds are an effective alternative to curtains. The choice of fabrics will make a difference to the look and hang of the blind. A heavy fabric is best kept to really large windows; voiles, sheers and soft cottons are all effective at small windows.

A blind can be used in place of a curtain, or a sheer blind can be used close to the window and curtains overhang. It can be extremely effective to have a mock blind at the top of the window as a decorative pelmet.

Festoon blinds are those which are gathered all the time, even when they are dropped down. Austrian blinds are gathered when raised but look like curtains when dropped. Both festoon and Austrian blinds will need fabric twice the width of the window. The blinds can be plain or frilled on the bottom edge, depending on the effect required. Kits for both types can be purchased at most good stores.

Roller blinds can be made up by purchasing the blind kit and using your own fabric. Alternatively, buy a plain blind and appliqué or embroidery on it. Roller blinds can be thick for keeping out the light, or they can be sheer and used as a screen rather than a light excluder. A roller blind is a very cost-effective way to dress a window, as the minimum of fabric is required.

Roman blinds also save on fabric. Again, kits can be purchased and are easy to follow. With a Roman blind the window dressing is softer when the blind is raised than with a roller blind, as the pleats softly pelmet the window.

◆ HOW TO MAKE AN AUSTRIAN BLIND ◆

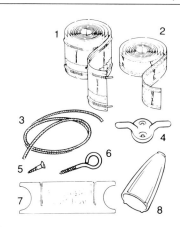

Contents
1 Nelpleat tape*
2 Austrian blind tape*
3 Austrian blind cord*
4 Brass cleat*
5 Brass cleat screws
6 Brass screw eyes*
7 Cord tidy*
8 Blind acorn
*Also available separately.

Kit
The Rufflette Austrian Blind Kit has been introduced to provide everything that you require for making a blind, apart from fabric, thread and batten. It is available in two sizes – Size 1 for windows 4–6 ft (120–180 cm) wide × 6 ft (180 cm) drop and Size 2 for windows 6-8 ft (180–245 cm) wide × 6 ft (180 cm) drop.

Two tapes are included in the kit, Netpleat for the heading and Austrian Blind Tape with the Cord to actually create the ballooning folds of the blind.

Netpleat is a pencil pleat heading tape which can be used without curtain hooks on a rod or stretchwire or in the conventional way on a curtain track.

Austrian Blind Tape dispenses with the need for curtain rings-saving both time and money. Both tapes are translucent which means they can be used unobtrusively on nets as well as fabrics.

Instructions
1 Carefully measure the window and cut the fabric to the drop plus 45 cm (18 in), allowing twice the width.

2 Join widths of fabric where necessary using a flat open seam. Hem the bottom and both sides of the fabric, or attach a frill of matching fabric for a pretty effect.

3 Turn and press a 3 mm (⅛ in) hem at the top of the blind. Sew Rufflette Netpleat Tape (the widest tape) to the wrong side, making sure that the hook pockets are both facing you and at the bottom of the tape. Knot and turn under one edge of the tape. Turn under but leave the cords free at the other edge.

4 For ease of sewing, fold the fabric concertina fashion every 60 cm (2 feet) and press. Open out and you will have straight guidelines for sewing. Sew vertical lines of Rufflette Austrian Blind Tape (the narrow tape) 2.5 cm (1 in) in from the edges of the wrong side of the fabric and at regular intervals of approximately 60 cm (2 feet). This measurement will obviously depend on how the width of the fabric divides equally. Ensure that any joins in the fabric are covered by a length of tape. Each length of tape should have a horizontal loop right at the bottom of the blind.

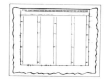

5 Draw up the cords of the heading tape to fit the width of the window. Do not cut off the surplus cords as these allow the blind to be pulled flat for laundering. Wind the cords round the Rufflette Cord Tidy provided: if using a curtain track, place Rufflette Standard Tape Hooks (R5) every 8 cm (3 in) (enclosed with Rufflette Austrian Blind Track) or use the special loops on the tape if the blind is being suspended from stretchwire or rod.

6 Fix a batten at the top of the window and insert the screw eyes, positioning them at the top of each vertical tape. The insertion of screw eyes in not necessary if using Rufflette Austrian Blind Track.

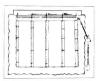

7 Mount the cleat to the wall beside the blind, using the two brass screws.

8 Start at the opposite end of the blind to the cleat, thread the cord through all the loops on the first vertical tape starting at the bottom loop and knotting (use the threader supplied with the Austrian Blind Track if purchased). Repeat this process with each vertical tape, then fix blind to track if one is being used, or alternatively onto a rod or stretchwire. Thread cords through the screw eyes, leaving enough cord hanging so that it can easily be reached to operate the blind. Plait the cords together, inserting the blind acorn over the cord ends for a neat appearance. These cords will be wound around the cleat when the blind is not being operated.

◆ HOW TO MAKE A ROMAN BLIND ◆

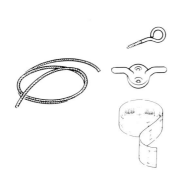

Materials

1 Fabric. To fit both the width of the window plus 5 cm (2 in) for side hems and the window drop, plus 7.5 cm (3 in) for top and bottom hems.

2 Rufflette Austrian Blind Tape. The length of the blind plus 1.5 cm (½ in) for turnings multiplied by the number of vertical tapes required. A length of tape down each side of the blind and at approximately every 40 cm (15 in) intervals is required.

3 Rufflette Austrian Blind Cord. Approximately double the amount of Rufflette Austrian Blind Tape.

4 Screw eyes (one for each vertical tape).

5 Narrow batten or dowling for hem of blind and batten for fixing.

6 Cleat.

7 Small tacks.

8 Matching thread.

Instructions

1 Cut fabric to fit your window allowing for hems. Join widths where necessary with a flat fell seam.

2 Sew side hems, turn and sew a 2.5 cm (1 in) top hem.

3 Turn and sew a 5 cm (2 in) bottom hem, but leaving one side open to take the batten or dowling.

4 With the wrong side of the fabric facing you, sew vertical lines of Rufflette Austrian Blind Tape 2.5 cm (1 in) in from the edges at regular intervals of approximately 40 cm (15 in). This measurement will obviously depend on how the width of your fabric divides equally. *Note:* The Austrian Blind Tape has horizontal loops woven into it at regular intervals-it is most important that each row of tape begin at the bottom with one of these loops.

6.35 Roman blind in Liberty cotton makes interesting use of stripes by Myra (McCabe)

5 To improve the operation of your blind starting with the second loop from the botton sew 3 mm (⅛ in) horizontal tucks, corresponding with every other loop, across the width of the blind on the right side of the fabric. This will help to form the tailored folds evenly.

6 Lay the almost completed blind right side down on a table, place the mounting batten at the top of the blind and tack the fabric to it.

7 Insert screw eyes into the batten and position them at the top of each vertical tape.

8 Mount the cleat on the wall at a suitable height for operating the blind.

9 Starting at the opposite end of the blind to the cleat, thread the cord through every other loop on the first vertical tape, starting at the bottom loop and knotting securely. Then thread through the screw eyes, leaving enough cord hanging so that it will reach the cleat. Repeat this process with each vertical tape, then plait the cords together. These cords will be wound around the cleat when the blind is not being operated.

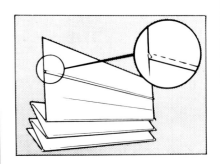

HEADING TAPES AND TRACKS

A good selection of heading tape is available to create just the desired effect for your window.

Full curtains with regular pencil pleats are achieved with Regis tape, which gives a crisp and upright heading. This style requires 2¼–2½ times fullness, and with two rows of pockets can be used on any type of curtain track or pole. It is suitable for most weights of fabric.

Tervoil is a pencil pleat tape especially designed for use with lightweight fabrics – sheers and nets. A fullness of 2¼–2½ times is re-quired, but static nets and sheers look best with 3 times the width.

Netpleat is another tape for nets and sheers; it is translucent. It creates pencil pleats and can be used with track, rod or stretched wire.

Tridis tape is used to form fanned triple pleats (pinch pleats). Always elegant, this heading is obtained simply by pulling two cords! Tridis requires double fullness, and can be used on any type of track or pole. It is suitable for all weights of fabrics, sheers and nets.

Deep Tridis is similar to Tridis, but deeper (5½ in) and so is ideal for full-length curtains. Make up as for Tridis. Tridis 40 is a narrow tridis, and so is suitable for very small windows and drops.

Cartridge pleats provide a pleasing tailored cylindrical pleat, and a gain merely by pulling up two draw cords. Cartridge tape requires double fullness and gives superb full-length drapes. It is suitable for all types of tracks and poles, and for any fabric, sheers or net.

Standard tape is approx. 1 in wide, and provides a pretty gathered heading which can be easily adjusted. This tape requires 1½–2 times fullness, and can be used on all weights of fabric. Standard tape is ideally used for curtains behind a pelmet or valance, but is equally good for valances and various frilled trims and tiebacks.

Standard Supreme tape will provide gathers or cluster pleats. Dainty tape is a merc 5/8 in wide. It is ideal for use on tiny windows or where a particularly small gather is required.

As a finishing touch, lining tape can be most helpful. Loose-lined curtains can be suitable if a particularly heavy fabric is used for the curtaining. The linings are slipped in behind and are easily detachable for extra laundering.

Lining tape can be particularly useful in bathrooms. A normal furnishing fabric can be used for a shower curtain, with a plastic lining to protect it from the water. Loose linings can also provide extra winter warmth, and are then easily removed in summer.

6.36 Deep tridis on Liberty Chintz by Myra (McCabe)

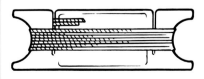

6.37 Rufflette cord tidy

◆ REGIS, TERVOIL AND NETPLEAT ◆

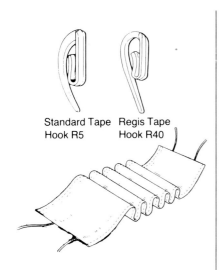

Standard Tape   Regis Tape
Hook R5   Hook R40

The sewing instructions for Netpleat are the same as those which follow. However, Netpleat has only one row of suspension pockets so if the tape is to cover the curtain track or if using stretchwire, sew with the pockets at the bottom. If the tape is to suspend below the track, sew with the pockets at the top. Use only the Standard Tape Hooks R5.

Sewing
1 Taking the edge of the tape that will come to the centre of the track (remember you will require a left and right hand curtain) pull out 4 cm (1½ in) of each cord and knot.

2 Trim off surplus tape 3 mm (⅛ in) from knots. Turn under the edge for neatness.

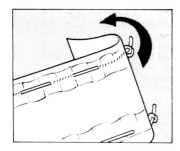

3 At the opposite edge of the tape pull free 3–5 cm (1–2 in) of the cords for eventual pleating of the curtain.

4 Turn under this second edge of the tape for neatness. Turn under and press a 6 mm (¼ in) hem at the top of the curtain. Ensure that the tape is the correct way up – yellow line at the bottom – and that the hook pockets are facing you. Machine the tape to the curtain along the turquoise sewing lines, leaving 3 mm (⅛ in) between the top of the tape and the top of the curtain. The top and bottom rows must be stitched in the same direction. Be careful not to sew over the cords.

Sew both side edges of the tape, but do not sew over the free cords for pleating.

Pleating
1 To pleat the curtain hold the free cords in one hand or with extra wide curtains loop them round a door handle. Gently push the heading along the cords until all the fabric is pleated to its maximum – this preforms the pleats. Ease the heading out again to the desired width, tie a slip knot to hold.

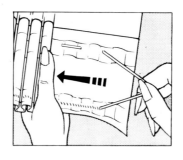

2 Do not cut off surplus cords as they allow the curtain to be pulled flat for cleaning. Loose cords should be wound neatly out of sight on a Rufflette Cord Tidy.

3 Using only the Regis Tape Hooks R40, insert at each end of the tape and approximately every 8 cm (3 in) along the curtain.

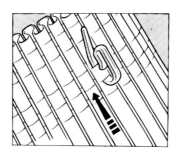

4 When attaching loose linings the Regis Hook is placed firstly through the buttonhole of the lining tape then through the pocket on the tape and turned over in the normal manner.

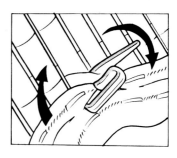

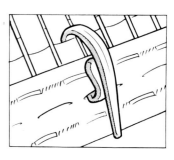

If you wish to suspend the curtains below the track use the top row of pockets for the curtain hooks. But if you require the track to be covered, the bottom row should be used.

◆ TRIDIS, DEEP TRIDIS AND TRIDIS 40 ◆

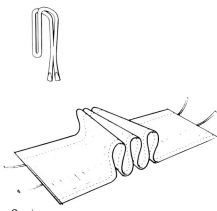

Sewing

1 Taking the edge of the tape that will come to the centre of the track, cut in the centre of a group of pleats (to free cords for knotting). Remember you will require a left and right hand curtain.

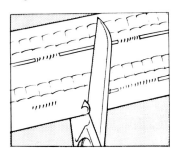

2 Pull free the cords to where they emerge. Knot each free cord and trim to within 3 mm (⅛ in) of the knots.

3 If you have an overlap arm on the track turn under 4 cm (1½ in) of tape. If the curtains butt together at the centre of the track, turn under 9 cm (3½ in) of tape.

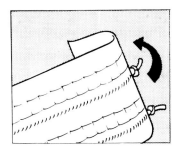

4 At the opposite edge of the tape pull out 3–5 cm (1–2 in) of cords for eventual pleating of the curtain. If the cords are not exposed, use the point of your scissors to pick them free from the channel of the tape for neatness.

5 Turn and press a 6 mm (¼ in) hem at the top of your curtain ensure that the tape is the correct way up-yellow line at the bottom-and that the hook pockets are facing you. Machine the tape to the curtain along the turquoise sewing lines, leaving 3 mm (⅛ in) between the top of the tape and the top of the curtain. The top and bottom rows must be stitched in the same direction. Be careful not to sew over the cords. Sew both side edges of the tape, but do not sew over the free cords for pleating.

Pleating

1 It is very important to pleat up the curtain correctly and to avoid puckering between the pleats. Hold the free cords in one hand or loop them round a door handle. Position fingers as indicated. Push first set of pleats into position and advance to second set also pushing them into position – now return to first set as these will no longer be pleated and advance and return along the curtain until the whole curtain is pleated. Tie a slip knot to hold.

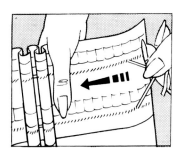

2 Do not cut off surplus cords as they allow the curtain to be pulled flat for cleaning. Loose cords should be wound neatly out of sight on a Rufflette Cord Tidy.

3 Using the special Tridis/Cartridge Tape Hooks R10, fit by inserting the two prongs into each of the two adjacent pockets at the back of each set of pleats and into adjacent pockets at each end of the curtain.

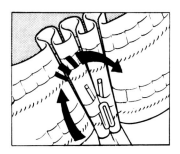

4 When attaching loose linings, a single prong of the Tridis/Cartridge Hook is placed through the buttonhole in the Lining Tape then each prong is inserted into the Tridis Tape as previously described.

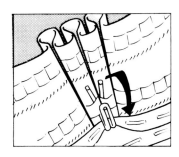

5 The pleating effect of Tridis Tape will be improved if a small tack is used to pinch the base of each pleat.

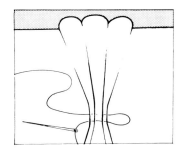

If you wish to suspend the curtains below the track use the top row of pockets for the curtain hooks. If you require the track to be covered, the bottom row should be used.

◆ CARTRIDGE PLEAT ◆

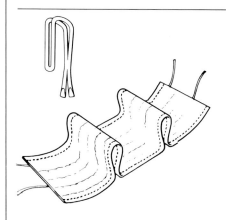

Sewing

1 Taking the edge of the tape that will come to the centre of the track, cut in the centre of the first pleat (to free cords for knotting). Remember you will require a left and right hand curtain.

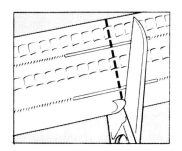

2 Knot each free cord then trim tape to within 3 mm (⅛ in) of the knots.

3 If the track has an overlap arm, turn under 2.5 cm (1 in) at the end of the tape including the knotted cords. However, if the curtains are to butt together at the centre of the track, turn under 5 cm (2 in) of the tape.

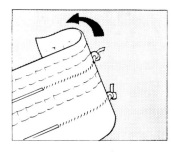

4 At the other end of the tape pull free 3–5 cm (1–2 in) of the cords for eventual pleating of the curtain. If the cords are not exposed, use the point of your scissors to pick them free from the channel of the tape.

5 Turn under each edge of the tape for neatness. Turn and press a 6 mm (¼ in) hem at the top of your curtain. Ensure that the tape is the correct way up – yellow line at the bottom – and that the hook pockets are facing you. Machine the tape to the curtain along the turquoise sewing lines, leaving 3 mm (⅛ in) between the top of the tape and the top of the curtain. The top and bottom rows must be stitched in the same direction. Be careful not to sew over the cords. Sew both side edges of the tape, but do not sew over the free cords for pleating.

Pleating

1 It is very important to pleat up the curtain correctly and to avoid puckering between the pleats. Hold free cords in one hand or loop them round a door handle. Position fingers as indicated. Push first set of pleats into position and advance to second set also pushing them into position – now return to first set as these will no longer be pleated and advance and return along the curtain until the whole curtain is pleated. Tie a slip knot to hold.

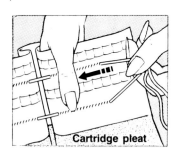

Cartridge pleat

2 Do not cut off surplus cords as they allow the curtain to be pulled flat for cleaning. Loose cords should be wound neatly out of sight on a Rufflette Cord Tidy.

3 Fit the special Tridis/Cartridge Tape Hooks R10, by inserting the two prongs into each of the two adjacent pockets at either side of the pleats. Also place one hook at each end of the curtain by inserting each prong of the hook into adjacent pockets.

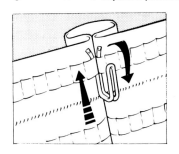

If the curtain finishes with a large flap of unpleated material an adjusting pleat can be formed by inserting each prong of the hook into two pockets about 10 cm (4 in) apart.

4 We recommend that the top of each Cartridge Pleat is filled with tissue paper, or similar soft substance (as used in custom-made headings of this type) to give each pleat a rounded fullness.

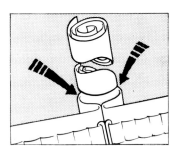

5 When attaching loose linings, a single prong of the Tridis/Cartridge Hook is placed through the buttonhole in the Lining Tape then each prong is inserted into the Cartridge Pleat Tape as previously described.

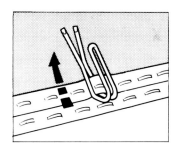

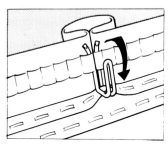

If you wish to suspend the curtains below the track use the top row of pockets for the curtain hooks. But if you require the track to be covered, the bottom row should be used.

◆ STANDARD SUPREME, STANDARD AND DAINTY ◆

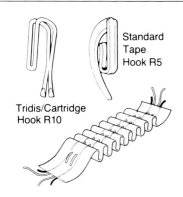

Standard
Tape
Hook R5

Tridis/Cartridge
Hook R10

The sewing instructions for Standard and Dainty are basically the same as those which follow for Standard Supreme. There is only one pair of gathering cords for Standard and Dainty which is the same as the inner pair on Standard Supreme. Use the following instructions remembering you only have one pair of gathering cords. To pleat either heading follow the instructions given for gathered headings.

Sewing
1 Taking the edge of the tape that will come to the centre of the track cut in the centre of a group of outer pleats (to free the cords for knotting). Remember you will re-quire a left and right hand curtain.

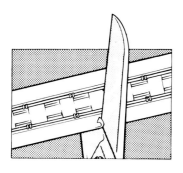

2 Pull free the outer cords to where they emerge and also pull free the inner cords to the same point. Knot each cord individually and trim to within 3 mm (⅛ in) of the knots.

3 If you have an overlap arm on your track, turn under 4 cm (1½ in) of tape. However if the curtains butt together at the centre of your track turn under 9 cm (3½ in) of tape (this last instruction only applies if you wish to use the cluster pleat effect).

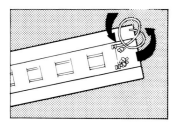

4 At the opposite edge of the tape pull out 3–5 cm (1–2 in) of cords for eventual pleat-ing of the curtain. If the outer cords are not exposed, use the point of your scissors to pick them free from the channel of the tape for neatness.

5 Turn and press a 4 cm (1½ in) hem at the top of the curtain, remembering to turn under the edges of the tape to neaten. Pin tape to curtain leaving 2.5 cm (1 in) between the top of the tape and the top of the curtain.

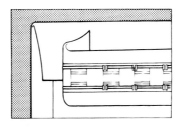

6 Now machine the tape to the fabric, avoiding cords and ensuring that both the top and bottom rows of stitching follow the same direction.

Cluster pleats
1 It is very important to pleat the curtain correctly and to avoid puckering between the clusters of pleats. Hold the free outer cords in one hand, or, with extra wide cur-tains loop them round a door handle. Posi-tion your thumb just in front of the first group of cluster pleats and gently push this

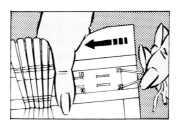

set of pleats into position, then advance to the second group of pleats also pushing them into position. Now return to the first set as these will no longer be pleated and advance and return along the curtain until all the pleats are in position. Tie a slip knot to hold then wind loose cords round a Rufflette Cord Tidy.

2 Using the special Tridis/Cartridge Hooks R10, fit by inserting the two prongs into each of the centre two adjacent pockets at the back of each set of pleats and also into adjacent pockets at each end of the curtain.

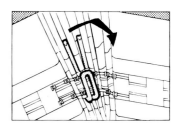

Gathered headings
1 To pleat the curtain, hold the free inner cords in one hand, or, with extra wide cur-tains loop them round a door handle. Gently push the heading along the cords until all the fabric is pleated to its maximum. Now ease the heading out again to the desired width, tie a slip knot to hold then wind loose cords round a Rufflette cord Tidy.

2 Using only Standard Tape Hooks R5, in-sert at each end of the curtain and approx-imately every 8 cm (3 in) along the curtain.

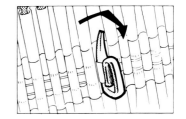

◆ LINING TAPE ◆

Sewing

1 Prepare the lining by joining widths where necessary with flat open seams and making side hems (these can be machined).

2 Pull out 4 cm (1½ in) of the two cords at one edge of the tape and knot together. Trim off surplus tape-this edge will come to the centre of the track-as with curtains a left and right lining must be made.

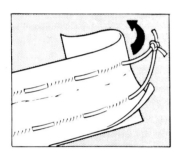

3 Place the top raw edge of the lining material between the two 'skirts' of the Lining Tape with cord side uppermost. The

Lining Tape should be slightly longer than the fabric width, so that it overlaps at each edge.

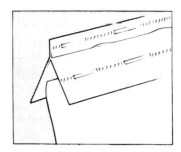

4 Turn under the overlapping edge of the tape so that it is level with the end of the fabric, stitch across this folded edge to neaten and secure. Machine along the bottom of the tape thus trapping the lining between the two 'skirts' of the tape. The underside of the 'skirt'is slightly longer than the corded side to ensure that the stitching will not miss it when sewing unseen. Finish the other edge of the tape in a similar manner, but leaving cords free for pleating the lining.

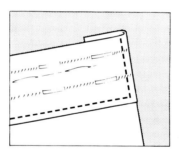

Pleating

1 Pleat up the lining by gently pushing the fabric along the cords to its maximum. Now pull out the lining to the width of the curtain it is to fit. Loose cords should be wound neatly out of sight on a Rufflette Cord Tidy.

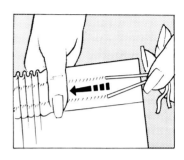

2 For a better finish, the edges of the lining and the curtain can be anchored together with a few tacks or a running thread.

◆ CURTAIN POLES AND TRACKS

A wide variety of tracks and poles is available. Many can be used with cording sets for easy pulling and to help protect your curtain fabric. Another simple pulling device is the wand, which is attached to the last runner; this is useful at smaller windows.

Tracks and poles must also complement the size and shape of the window and be suitable for the type of heading tape you have chosen.

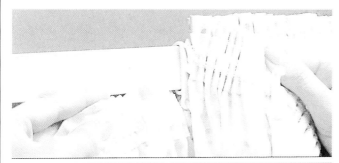

6.39 **Swish Nylonglyde track and valance**

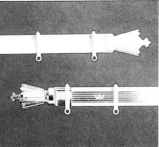

6.38 **Swish Sologlyde – versatile and flexible**

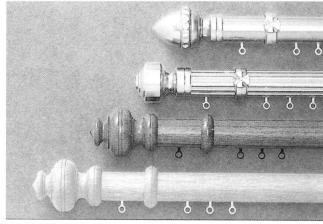

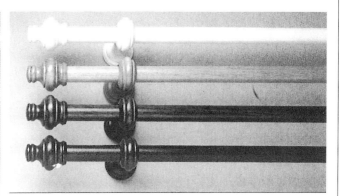

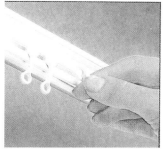

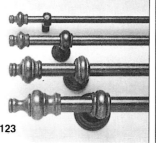

123

6.41 **Swish wooden poles – for curtains, towel rails and bedheads**

6.40 **Swish Novapoles look like a pole but work like a track**

Tootal threads, haberdashery, scissors, cutting boards and so on are available from major department stores and specialist retailers.

Vilene interfacings are available from major department stores, fabric retailers and other specialist outlets.

Invisible (concealed) zippers are available from John Lewis Stores, House of Fraser Stores, Lewis Ltd, and some specialist retailers.

An invisible zipper foot is available to fit many makes and models from Machine Craft, 59 Bridge Lanes Hebden Bridge, West Yorkshire.

Liberty fabrics are available through major stores and specialist retailers, including Liberty shops throughout the UK.

Alexander fabrics are in Wentworth Street, London E1 and also in Epsom, Surrey and in Bexleyheath, Kent.

Rufflet and Swish products are available from department stores, many specialist furnishing and curtaining retailers, and interior design studios.

A specialist supplier of threads, haberdashery, sewing equipment, interfacings and specialist fabrics, by mail order or personal call, is: MacCulloch and Wallis Ltd, 25/6 Dering Street, London W1R 0BH.

Leather skins and pieces, buckles, clasps etc. are available to personal callers and mail order from A. L. Maugham and Co Ltd, 5 Faza-kerbey street, Liverpool L3 9DN.

All the sewing machines are available from department stores or specialist sewing machine retailers, and it is recommended that you receive expert tuition and advice upon purchase.

Repairs and service to sewing machines can be obtained from the department store where the purchase was made or from a qualified mechanic/retailer. The Sewing Machine Traders Association is the trade association to which most reputable dealers belong.

There is a full list of company names and addresses at the front of this book. They will supply further information on any product, and the names of retailers in your area.